BeesKnees #5:
A Beekeeping Memoir:

Volume Five: Days 401 - 500

The Journey of a Beginning Beekeeper

Fran Stewart

BeesKnees #5: A Beekeeping Memoir
Fran Stewart
© 2020

All rights reserved. No part of this book may be used or reproduced in any manner whatsoever without written permission from the author, except by a reviewer who may quote brief passages in a review.

Cover design by Darlene Carter

ISBN: 978-1-951368-05-0

This book was printed in the United States of America.

Published by
My Own Ship Press
PO Box 490153
Lawrenceville GA 30049

myownship@icloud.com
franstewart.com

To those who love bees and cats and all living things

Books by Fran Stewart

The Biscuit McKee Mystery Series:

Orange as Marmalade
Yellow as Legal Pads
Green as a Garden Hose
Blue as Blue Jeans
Indigo as an Iris
Violet as an Amethyst
Gray as Ashes

Red as a Rooster
Black as Soot
Pink as a Peony
White as Ice

A Slaying Song Tonight

The Scot Shop Mysteries:

A Wee Murder in My Shop
A Wee Dose of Death
A Wee Homicide in the Hotel

Poetry:

Resolution

For Children:

As Orange As Marmalade/
    Tan naranja como Mermelada
      (a bilingual book)

Non-Fiction:

From The Tip of My Pen: a workbook for writers
BeesKnees #1: A Beekeeping Memoir
BeesKnees #2: A Beekeeping Memoir
BeesKnees #3: A Beekeeping Memoir
BeesKnees #4: A Beekeeping Memoir
BeesKnees #5: A Beekeeping Memoir

Introduction to BeesKnees #5

When you get to Day # 474, you'll see that I gave up journaling on a daily basis when I started writing my BeesKnees blog. It seemed like a duplicate effort—plus the blog was more interesting than the poorly inspired journaling I'd been doing.

Once this beekeeping blog was complete, though, I went back to journaling every day. Then, several years ago, I began posting every morning on my Facebook author page—FranStewartAuthor—and realized that both the BeesKnees blog and my FB pages were memoirs in that they showed what my daily life was like—what was important to me, what I was dealing with, what I was thinking about. That's why I've chosen to publish BeesKnees for future generations, and why my next project will be to publish FranStewartAuthor. I just need to come up with a good title for it.

I do hope you're enjoying this journey with me.

>--Fran
>from my house beside a creek
>on the other side of Hog Mountain GA

Fran Stewart

Day #401 Oh Oh Oh!
See Spot Run! Bees Are Smart!
Thursday, November 17, 2011

You know, if we humans were judged on our ability to breathe underwater (without the benefit of SCUBA), we'd all fail.

It seems that scientists have just recently discovered that bees know how to fly efficiently and how to find the best possible routes to and from nectar sources, despite the fact that their little bee brains are "the size of a grass seed."

I'm quoting an article posted last month on TG Daily by David Gomez.

The title should have warned me what was to come: **"Bee brains calculate better than expensive computers"**

Do tell.

"Bees could now be in the running for the title of most efficient being known to man. A new study has found that our honey producing friends are better at mathematical functions than today's most powerful computers."

Gomez, it appears, was expounding on an article in Natural News. I went to the source and found this ending paragraph:

"Previous studies have found that bees have amazing memory capacities for their size. Their incredible olfactory senses are also amazingly powerful at discerning and remember[sic] different smells and aromas."

The article could have used a good editor. Besides having questionable grammar in that second sentence, aren't smells and aromas pretty much the same thing?

Still, it is nice to know officially that bees can navigate and smell. Just how did those scientists think bees have been finding flowers for millions of years?

BeesKnees #5: A Beekeeping Memoir

The study, according to Natural News, says "bees are able to quickly calculate the shortest flying routes among their network of flowers and plants in order to minimize flying time, a feat that even the speediest computers take days to solve."

The reason for the study? So computers will be able to figure out how to route traveling salesmen in the most efficient ways. Of course, what they don't take into account is that bees can travel in relatively straight lines, dodging around trees and soaring over buildings. Traveling salesmen will never be able to travel like that.

Gomez condescends to admit that "The intelligence paradigm for small creatures has changed. Studies have found that bees ... have amazingly powerful brains for their diminutive size. Animals that we once thought to be simple are turning out to be far more complex than anyone could have imagined."

Excuse me, Mr. Gomez? Bees have been around for more than 140 million years. They are the only insect that produces food that is good for humans. They produce it whether or not humans are around to steal the honey from them. They produce honey still, despite the fact that we as a race are polluting their world. Who's this "we" who once thought bees to be simple?

Bees – simple? Ha! Those scientists should have read my blog for the past 400 days.

BeeAttitude for Day #401: *Blessed are those who study (and appreciate) the wonder around us, for they shall live in awe of Mother.*

p.s. from Fran – I truly am glad that people are discovering the wonder of honeybees. Just had to vent a bit at the tone.

Fran Stewart

 ***Day #402 Lincoln Logs and Honey Combs***
Friday, November 18, 2011

One of my favorite toys when I was a kid was an old set of Lincoln Logs. I could spend hours creating towers and paddocks, houses and barns, fences and factories. Even to this day, I'm happy when I'm swinging a hammer, putting together a set of honey supers.

Is the propensity to build an innate yearning? My grandson Aiden was here the other day. He pulled out the set of Dominos I keep in an old oatmeal box. With quiet intensity he built and built.

First it was a fenced corral for the domino horses. Then it was a hotel. Finally a tower with a microwave doohickey on top and a crowded parking lot below.

BeesKnees #5: A Beekeeping Memoir

Bees build honeycomb. Kids build towers and parking lots. Grannies build (sometimes lopsided) trellises and planters.

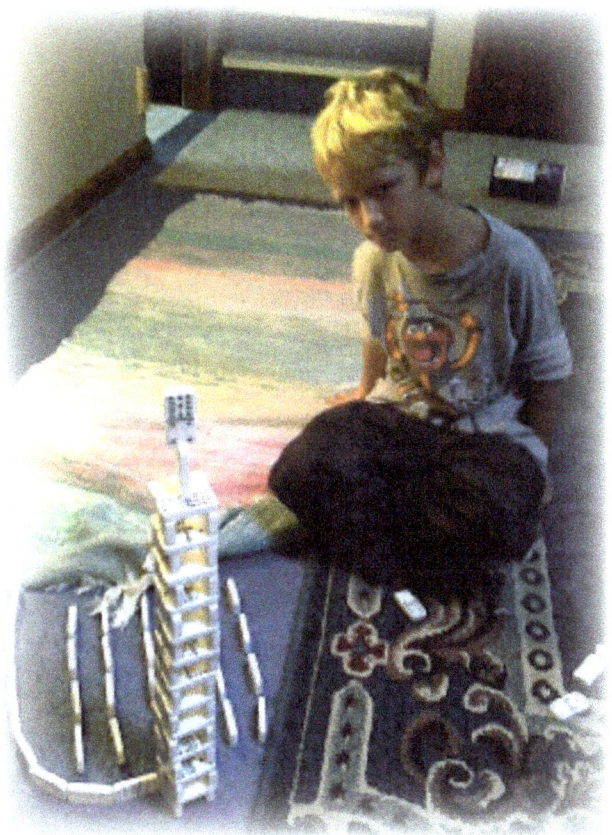

I've never heard of bees taking down what they built. I'll have to do some research. What happens if a honeycomb isn't well anchored? Do they just wait for it to collapse under its own weight, the way my grandson's third tower keeled over when it was 27 dominoes high? Or do they somehow or other reverse the building process, chew up the wax, spit it out, and start over again?

I don't know. Do you?

BeeAttitude for Day #402: *Blessed are those who ask questions and try to find the answers, for they shall remain interested in life all their days.*

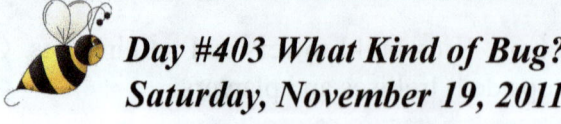

Day #403 What Kind of Bug?
Saturday, November 19, 2011

Does anyone know what kind of bug this is?

These guys really enjoyed camping out on my Aesclepias (Butterfly Weed) all summer. Once the flowers went to seed, they decided my mailbox was the perfect meeting place. Nobody else on my street has them. Of course, nobody else on my street has as many flowers as I do, particularly not the Aesclepias.

I was outside a couple of days ago before the rain started, and was lectured by my mail carrier about those "creepy bugs."

They're kinda cute. They don't bite. They don't seem to eat anything that I don't want eaten. And they keep each other company. What's creepy about that?

I just wish I could identify them. Can you help?

[**2019 Note:** See Day #407 for the answer.]

BeeAttitude for Day #403: *Blessed are those who laugh hard every day, for their hearts shall beat joyously.*

BeesKnees #5: A Beekeeping Memoir

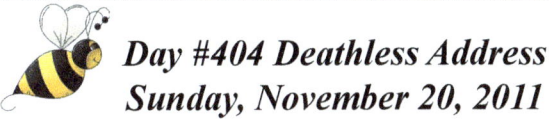

Day #404 Deathless Address
Sunday, November 20, 2011

Yesterday was the 148th anniversary of the Gettysburg Address.

Lord, what I wouldn't give to be able to write something even half that memorable. It seems apt to post the text—although I probably should have done it yesterday, but yesterday I was busy wondering about bugs.

You probably had to memorize this speech when you were in high school. But do you ever pull it out and think about what it's saying? This is a lot like the Declaration of Independence, one of those documents we know about, approve of, but seldom consider at any depth. I read the Declaration of Independence every Fourth of July, as I've mentioned before in this blog. I think it would make sense for me to read Lincoln's words every November 19th from now on. I'm gonna do it. Will you join me, even if we're a day late this year?

= = = = = = = = = =

Four score and seven years ago our fathers brought forth on this continent a new nation, conceived in liberty, and dedicated to the proposition that all men are created equal.

Now we are engaged in a great civil war, testing whether that nation, or any nation, so conceived and so dedicated, can long endure. We are met on a great battlefield of that war. We have come to dedicate a portion of that field, as a final resting place for those who here gave their lives that that nation might live. It is altogether fitting and proper that we should do this.

But, in a larger sense, we can not dedicate, we can not consecrate, we can not hallow this ground. The brave men, living and dead, who struggled here, have consecrated it, far above our poor power to add or detract.

The world will little note, nor long remember what we say here, but it can never forget what they did here. It is for us the living, rather, to be dedicated here to the unfinished work which they who fought here have thus far so nobly advanced. It is rather for us to be here dedicated to the great task remaining before us—that from these honored dead we take increased devotion to that cause for which they gave the last full measure of devotion—that we here highly resolve that these dead shall not have died in vain—that this nation, under God, shall have a new birth of freedom—and that government of the people, by the people, for the people, shall not perish from the earth.

= = = = = = = = = =

BeeAttitude for Day #404: *Blessed are those who plant windbreaks for our hives, for they shall sleep well, knowing they've helped us bees to survive the winter.*

BeesKnees #5: A Beekeeping Memoir

 ***Day #405 Confederate Roses - Do Bees Read?***
Monday, November 21, 2011

While I was uploading my newest book, VIOLET AS AN AMETHYST, to turn it into an e-book, I got to wondering about that quote I featured last month on Day #379.

If we judged honeybees on their ability to read human texts, those poor little critters would fail miserably. But if we judged humans on their ability to read the nectar content of flowers – guess who the losers would be? That's right. All of us two-legged creatures.

Even though I read a number of draft chapters of VIOLET to my honeybees as I sat writing on my back deck, I doubt they appreciated the content. A number of them checked out my pencil, walked across my spiral bound notebook, and flew around my brain as it spewed words forth onto the page.

But, try as I might, I can't read what my girls are thinking as they delve into the five-inch-wide blossoms of the Confederate Roses (just about the last plant blooming in my yard this fall).

Incidentally, did you know the Confederate Rose is named after Rose O'Neal Greenhow, who was a spy during the War Between the States? Just one of those strange facts I pick up here and there.

At any rate, the point I'm trying to make is that I couldn't make any type of rose bloom or extract the nectar from it and create honey. Better not compare myself to bees or I'll get an inferiority complex – just like Day #379's fish.

BeeAttitude for Day #405: *Blessed are those who learn new skills and maintain old skills, for they shall face life with confidence.*

Day #406 When Bees Go Robbing
Tuesday, November 22, 2011

Yes, bees can be larcenous at times. If they find a weak hive, undefended by many guard bees, the stronger bees are quite liable to head inside and rob the stores of honey.

I can understand it in bees. It's called survival instinct.

I have less tolerance for humans who do that sort of thing. If you've tried to buy my e-books on Smashwords any time in the last two days, you'll notice that they're not there. What does this have to do with bees?

I'm glad you asked.

As I said, I can understand why bees would try to get away without paying for the honey they rob. But Smashwords.com has a policy of allowing anyone to download e-books with the understanding that they will be honorable and will pay for the books they download.

I was looking over my royalty statement from Smashwords and found that for every book someone bought (and they were only $3.99), between 50 and 80 people downloaded that same book without paying.

Now, I'm really happy that folks want to read my books, but why on earth would I want to put my books out there when there are only a few honest people who understand that writing is a job, one that supposedly supports the writer?

If you want to get my books for your non-Kindle, maybe there's a way you'll be able to find them, but until I can figure out a way to prevent the piracy, I'm going to leave my e-books off of Smashwords.

I'll let you know if I solve this quandary.

[**2019 Note:** I finally discovered a distributor who would format my e-books and send them out to all the regular channels, which means my e-books are now available to a whole lot more people and in a whole raft of formats I never have taken the time to figure out for myself. And, *except for Amazon,* I get paid fairly for all my e-books.]

BeeAttitude for Day #406: *Blessed are those who act in accordance with the highest thought, for they shall contribute to a better life for all.*

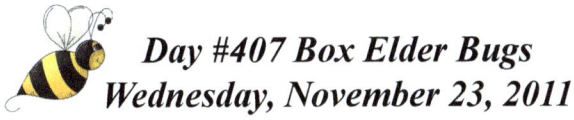

Day #407 Box Elder Bugs
Wednesday, November 23, 2011

What could be better than a day-before-Thanksgiving discussion of **bugs**?

Remember a few days ago when I asked if anyone could identify those red bugs on my mailbox? Well, Cathy Akers-Jordan responded saying they looked like Box Elder Bugs.

I don't have any Box Elder trees, but I went online and Googled the critters. The pictures I saw were mostly black with some orange-red stripes.

Nope. Not my bugs.

Or so I thought.

Cathy came back with a link to a website that has photos of Box Elder Bugs in all sorts of life stages,

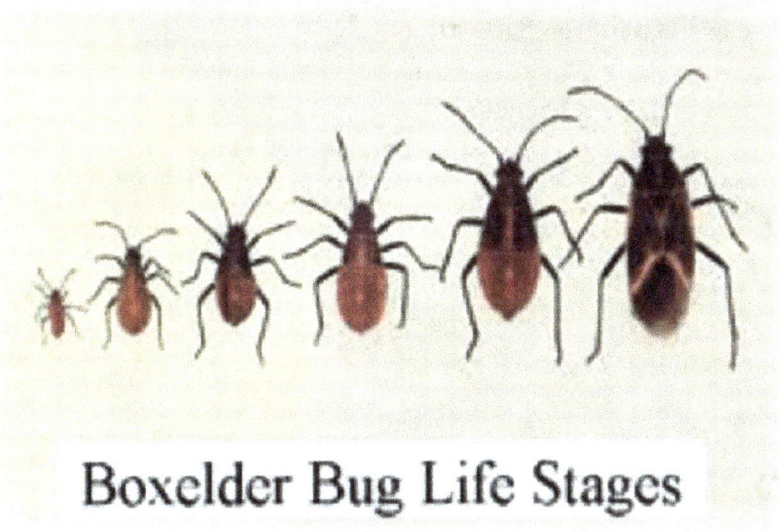

including one photo taken from underneath the bug, showing the little orange places on the thorax where the legs hinge onto the body. Cool huh?

Turns out my little orange guys are probably babies. When I looked more closely at my mailbox, I found some of those adults with their distinctive markings. Mine appear to be a variation on the usual kind, but there was plenty of diversity in those pictures that Cathy found.

So, I've learned that what I Google may not be the final answer.

You already knew that, though, didn't you?

BeeAttitude for Day #407: *Blessed are those who keep looking for nectar, for they shall eventually be satisfied.*

bee.s. from Fran - Have a joy-filled Thanksgiving Day tomorrow.

bee.s. from the bees: Have a joy-filled day *every* day.

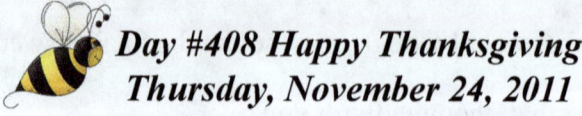

Day #408 Happy Thanksgiving
Thursday, November 24, 2011

It was so tempting to skip a few days of this blog. After all, this is a holiday, right?

Right.

But then, there's the discipline of a commitment. On October 12, 2010, I stated publicly that I would blog every single day for 600 days. And so far (SO FAR, indeed) I've done it. A little thing like a holiday shouldn't get in the way.

I just looked back through my blog posts for November of 2010, and I seem to have completely ignored Thanksgiving last year. I don't want to do that this year because this appears to be a year when we need all the thanks-giving we can come up with. And, after all, my personal mission statement is **"Healing the world through teaching the power of gratitude."**

But for today, I'm not going to do any teaching. I'm just going to tell you that this year I'm particularly thankful for you.

BeeAttitude for Day #408: *Blessed are those who live in the moment—the way we bees do—for they shall find much to be thankful for.*

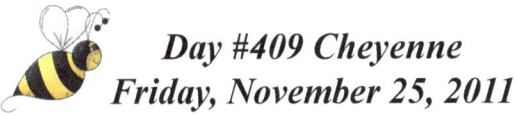 Day #409 Cheyenne
Friday, November 25, 2011

Whoops! Here it is the day after Thanksgiving, and now it appears to be time to head toward Christmas.

Well, in that spirit, I'd like to bring in the energy of Cheyenne, the official greeter at Wild Birds Unlimited in Suwannee, Georgia.

And here is Cheyenne:

Photo Credit Egor Kamelev (Pexels.com)

Whoops! That's not Cheyenne. That's the honeybee who brings you the BeeAttitudes in every BeesKnees blog post.

Cheyenne (shown below) is, as you may recall, the dog I wrote into A SLAYING SONG TONIGHT, and she did add, I must say, a delightful perspective to that book.

Fran Stewart

I'd like to encourage you to treat this holiday season with a laid-back, stress-free attitude. Right. Maybe I should say a more nearly laid-back and only minor-ly stressful attitude.

Act like a bee or like a dog. Appreciate life. Take one day at a time. Shake a few jingle bells, sip some eggnog, and join in the fun.

[2019 Note: Cheyenne crossed the Rainbow Bridge peacefully several months ago after a long and happy dog life. Her mom and dad miss her, and so do I. WBU just isn't the same without her wagging tail greeting me when I walk in the door. At least she lives on in Slaying Song. And in our memories.]

BeeAttitude for Day #409: *Blessed are those who find joy in the small details—well-made combs, active workers, a productive hive, and plenty of stores for the winter. What more does a bee—or a human—need?*

BeesKnees #5: A Beekeeping Memoir

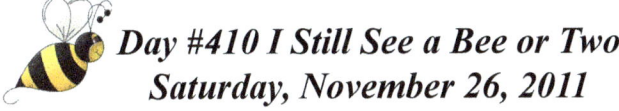 ## *Day #410 I Still See a Bee or Two*
Saturday, November 26, 2011

A couple of days ago the weather here in Georgia was warm enough to entice me outside to do some drastically overdue yard work. And there were some golden honeybees that kept me company as I weeded, dug up the vastly overgrown daylilies, and rescued several thousand (or so it seemed) crocus bulbs.

It won't be long before it will be way too cold for the bees to venture outside, and I must say I tend to emulate the bees. I spent twenty-six years living in Vermont, and although the winters are GORGEOUS there, I found that the longer I stayed—okay, what I'm really talking about is the older I got—the colder those winters seemed.

It didn't help that I had a malfunctioning thyroid, something I discovered after I moved to a warmer climate. I know I mentioned my thyroid way back on Day #13, but did I ever tell you about Jazzminka, the cat who **healed** my thyroid? If you know me and I already told you the story, just skip down to the BeeAttitude for the day.

Bees keep themselves warm in winter by shivering, rapidly contracting and un-contracting the muscles that usually power their wings, thereby creating heat. But people can't shiver enough to warm themselves like that. I've never figured out how to use my wing muscles, much less disconnect them.

People depend on the thyroid to regulate internal temperature, causing our body to generate more heat in the winter and less of it in the summer. (Obviously I'm greatly simplifying the process.) But when the thyroid doesn't function properly, temps get all screwed up.

I used to be so cold all winter long, it was downright painful.

Even when I moved to Georgia, with the fairly mild winters here, I still ached through the cold months and (maybe even worse) in the over-air-conditioned buildings in the summer. Brrr!

I discovered a doctor, though, who diagnosed hypothyroidism and who prescribed Synthroid, with the warning that once I started taking it, the Synthroid would destroy any remaining thyroid function and I would have to take Synthroid for the rest of my life.

I thought it was a small price to pay for the chance (finally!) to be warm. And I took the medication for several years, increasing it a bit each winter and backing off the dosage a bit each summer (per doctor's orders).

But then I brought **Jazzminka** into my home. She was a Humane Society kitten, a gray / black / white tabby who was way too young to be away from her mom. She used to give me hickies from sucking so long and so hard at the skin of my neck. I thought she was just missing her mommy.

As she grew, she began kneading the front of my neck—hard enough that it hurt. She was persistent, and would spend 20 or 30 minutes at it if I'd let her.

Gradually I found that the dosage of Synthroid seemed too high. The doc said to cut the pills in half. Eventually I had to quarter them. And finally I was taking a quarter of a pill every other day—and then every three days.

Jazzminka tapered off her insistence on kneading my thyroid as I got healthier, although she would still climb up and give me little "checkouts" occasionally. She died of a happy old age several years ago, fully knowing (I'm sure) that she had herded me through a healing process that I wouldn't have believed if I hadn't experienced it.

Since then, I've had my thyroid tested, and it's perfectly normal, so now I don't have to unhinge my wing muscles.

[**2019 Note:** In 2014 my thyroid acted up again, in the opposite direction, but that's a whole nother story. I wrote about it on my Facebook page FranStewartAuthor, and I'll include it in my regular memoirs if and when I get them published.]

BeeAttitude for Day #410: *Blessed are those who accept the gifts from Mama Nature, for she never leads us astray.*

Day #411 Drones Don't Have Daddies
Sunday, November 27, 2011

Isn't there a Grandparents' Day coming up soon? If so, drones (the male honeybees) will probably be delighted to celebrate it. After all, each drone has a grandfather.

But Father's Day? Drones don't have a dad to send a card to or buy a tie for.

How is this possible? I'm glad you asked.

I went to the Honeybee Research & Extension Lab website so I'd be sure the answer was scientifically valid. Here's what Ed Beary wrote:

The queen and workers are female bees with a diploid set of chromosomes. The drones are male with a haploid set of chromosomes. To get a female worker bee, the queen must add sperm to the egg. There must be a male to provide that sperm. To get a male, she does nothing but deposit the egg in a cell. No sperm in needed from a male bee.

[2019 Note: The website is still there, but I couldn't find this particular quote. I suppose that websites change as much as the population of a beehive—every six weeks there's a completely new set of worker bees since the others have all completed their life cycle. Or like the cells of our bodies – every seven years every single cell within us has died and been replaced. Something to think about.]

Photo Credit: UF/IFAS Honey Bee Research & Extension Lab

Maybe this is why drones are so relatively unproductive around the hive. They don't have a daddy to show them what work is supposed to be like.

Drones fulfill only three functions, as far as we people know. They:

- Grow up in a big drone cell that's been built around the outside edge of the hive so that if a bear tears open the hive, the bear is more likely to eat drone cells before it can destroy the center of the hive,

- Protect the queen on her mating flight by surrounding her and serving as bait for marauding birds, and finally,

- Mate with one queen (not necessarily the one from their own hive), and then they die.

If those are their only reasons for living, I'm not sure a daddy would help.

BeeAttitude for Day #411: *Blessed are those who know what they want to do when they grow up, for they shall get a head start on the rest of us.*

Day #412 Messiah Sing-Along
Monday, November 28, 2011

Yesterday was a special day for me. Every year, on the Sunday after Thanksgiving, the Gwinnett Choral Guild hosts a Messiah Sing-along. If people have scores, they bring them along. If not, the Guild has a bunch to loan out.

We, meaning the Choral Guild, and the BJ Chorale (co-hosts of the event) pay for professional singers to do the solo work, as well as a small chamber group and a couple of dynamic trumpeters (for the Hallelujah Chorus).

The audience sort of divides up into sections – Sopranos, Altos, Tenors, and Basses. And we sing out hearts out.

It's glorious! Now, as far as I'm concerned, the holidays are almost over. I've become something of a Grinch, as I've mentioned before. I still need to watch George C. Scott's Christmas Carol, sing one more concert with the Choral Guild this coming weekend, and send in an extra donation to Heifer International in my grandchildren's names; then that's quite enough holiday for me, and I am content.

[**2019 Note:** The Choral Guild folded several years ago, but the tradition of the sing-along continues. Now it's held each year on the Sunday <u>before</u> Thanksgiving.]

BeeAttitude for Day #412: *Blessed are those who celebrate joyously, for their hearts shall sing, just the ways our bee hearts buzz.*

Day #413 Rain, Rain, Rain and Wildfires
Tuesday, November 29, 2011

It's raining in Georgia. And that reminds me of a story. Today I'm going to tell you *my* version of it. Tomorrow I'll give you *my sister's* version.

My sister is quite a writer. She told me I could use an excerpt from an upcoming book of hers, *Farm Wife Stories*, which won't be published until some time or other – whenever she finishes writing it. I'll be sure to let you know when it's available. [**2019 Note:** *She's still working on it.*]

But, for now, here's what I remember.

Sixty some-odd years ago, Mississippi could have used some rain. I know, because that was the summer I spent at my grandparents' farm with my mother and my older sister. One day, one of the fields caught fire, and every available adult ran out to help save the crop and keep the fire from spreading to the house.

Our mother sat my sister and me in a big old chair, pointed a finger in our faces, and bent her stern face close to ours. "You sit there," she said, "and don't you move—not for any reason at all!"

We sat. I don't remember knowing exactly why we had to sit there, but I was with the big sister I idolized. I'm sure my sister was bored silly, and maybe even frightened, because I'm fairly certain she knew there was a fire going on, while I was blissfully ignorant of the implications of a wildfire. Our mother, meanwhile, was busy pounding at the flames with wet feed sacks.

So, when honeybees are faced with the smell of smoke (as they are each time a beekeeper smokes a hive before opening it), do they:

- sit blissfully unaware of what's happening around them, as I did? No.

- stay in one place and worry like my sister? No.

- do their best to fight the fire, the way Mama did? Not exactly.

You see, bees don't fight fire. They run from it. But first, they load up on honey so they can carry their food supply with them when they leave.

So today I sit here looking out at the rain which, as I write this, has been going on for more than 12 hours, thankful that I don't have to worry about fire. And thankful, too, that no enormous white-jacketed monster is coming around to blow smoke at me and lift the roof off my hive ... I mean my house.

Whew!

Just think of this – fish in the ocean never have to worry about wildfires. Whew again! They do, however, have to worry about the pollution we humans inflict upon them. How can we justify threatening sweet little faces like this one?

Photo Credit: Eli Reiman

Fran Stewart

Now, remember to check this blog tomorrow for my sister's side of the story.

BeeAttitude for Day #413: *Blessed are the rainmakers, for they shall save lives.*

Day #414 Farm Wife Story
Wednesday, November 30, 2011

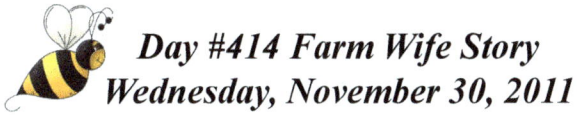

Yesterday, as I'm sure you recall, I promised to give my sister's side of the story about the fire on my Grandma's farm. I've talked about my sister before in this blog (on 11/20/10 and 9/25/11). She's an incredible fabric artist, who created a series of quilts and art pieces that **show** what depression feels like. Then she wrote a book about it: Depression Visible: the Ragged Edge.

Now she's writing another book (Farm Wife Stories) about what life is like on a wheat farm in eastern Colorado, from the point of view of the woman on that farm. She agreed to let me give you a taste of that book by quoting this little vignette of the same story I told, but from her point of view. This excerpt is from the introduction to Farm Wife Stories. As I mentioned yesterday, I'll let you know when the book is available.

= = = = = = = = = =

All the grownups were outside trying to put out the fire in the field across the road. We heard them shouting. They sounded scared. Was Mama okay? She said not to move, that she would come back for us. The windows were turning red now. I wondered if she would get burned up. No, she said she would be back.

I wrapped my arms around Fran and we sat there waiting and rocking until Fran said to quit because her tummy hurt.

We knew what they were doing because we had seen them before, slapping with the backs of shovels and wet gunnysacks at small fires they had set to burn weeds. My job was to take the sacks to the pump and rewet them as quick as I could and carry them dripping back to the grownups. But that was in the yard and during the daytime.

I wondered how they could keep the gunnysacks wet clear across the road. I could be out there helping them because I was the Big Sister. But Fran was still little. I had to stay in the chair with her. The red glow slowly turned dark, but Mama didn't come for a long time. We stayed in the chair, not getting out even to turn on the lights.

Finally she came. "What took so long?" I asked as she hugged us. "I had to stay," she answered, "to help put out all the little spots that were still burning. I'm glad you stayed here safe in the chair."

==========

It's funny that Diana writes, "We knew what they were doing." This half of that *we* hadn't a clue—or at least not one that I remember all these years later.

Do you have an older sister (or brother) who might have protected you at some time or other? Do you even remember it?

I'd encourage you to ask, today. After all, there's no telling what sort of great story you'll hear.

Thank you, Diana!

BeeAttitude for Day #414: *Blessed are the sisters, for they shall all work together to keep the hive healthy.*

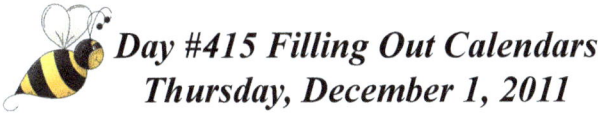
Day #415 Filling Out Calendars
Thursday, December 1, 2011

December is the month I always fill out my scheduling calendar for the upcoming year. It takes a while to do it, but I rather enjoy the ritual. Bees don't need calendars. They know what their schedule will be.

Queen:

Grow a bit

Fly out and mate with 30 or 40 drones

Lay eggs for the rest of my life.

Drone:

Fly along with the queen

Mate and croak

Workers:

Day 1   Clean out the cell I just hatched from; fly out to see where I live

Day 2   Clean out lots of other cells

Day 3   Clean more cells

Day 4   Feed some larvae

Day 5   Feed more larvae

Day 6   Feed more

Fran Stewart

Day 7 Collect garbage and dump it outside

Day 8 Drag more garbage outside

Day 9 Garbage duty

Day 10 Repair damaged comb

Day 11 Build some new comb

Day 12 Build comb

Day 13 Repair comb

Day 14 Build more comb

Day 15 Take nectar from incoming bees

Day 16 Put incoming pollen in cells

Day 17 Insert nectar in cells

Day 18 Food duty

Day 19 Fan the nectar to evaporate the water

Day 20 Fan nectar to evaporate the water

Day 21 Fan nectar to evaporate water

Day 22 Fan nectar – Whew!

Day 23 Stand guard to protect the hive

Day 24 Guard the front door

Day 25 Guard duty

Day 26 Fly around to orient myself

Day 27 Gather nectar and pollen

Day 28   Same thing

Day 29   and so on 'til the end of my life

I think I'd rather have my calendar.

BeeAttitude for Day #415: *Blessed are those who enjoy their work, for their smiles shall be radiant.*

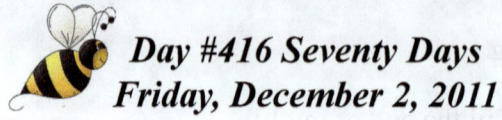

Day #416 Seventy Days
Friday, December 2, 2011

In a recent newspaper column, Lisa Earl McLeod mentioned the **1 percent rule** that she had picked up from her mentor, Alan Weiss:

"Instead of trying to be perfect at everything," she wrote, "pick something that's going to make a difference and make a vow to get 1 percent better at it every day."

According to Weiss, "If you improve by 1 percent each day, in 70 days you'll be twice as good."

The math for this may seem counter-intuitive. Wouldn't it take 100 days to increase by 100 percent?

Nope.

Say you're starting at a level of **12**, and you want to get to **24**. If you increase by 1% each day, the first day you'd go from 12 to 12.12,

- the second day from 12.12 to 12.2412,

- day 3 from 12.2412 to 12.363612, and so on.

- By day 9, you'd be at 13.12422327221233,

- and by day 35, you'd be just a hair under 17 (16.99923307237521).

Sure enough, on day 70, you'd accomplish your goal. In fact, you'd be a teeny bit over the mark (24.0811604207446).

Didn't you always want to know that?

Of course, you'd have to be diligent about that 1% improvement each day.

You can apply this to just about anything. Learn a bit more each day. Practice a bit more. Study a bit more. Walk a bit more.

BeesKnees #5: A Beekeeping Memoir

Wanna **move a mountain** / **write a book** / **become a beekeeper** / **learn Esperanto**? Now you know how.

BeeAttitude for Day #416: *Blessed are those who build their comb with steady work, for they shall have honey aplenty.*

Day #417 Telling it again and again
Saturday, December 3, 2011

It's funny how often I run into people who haven't heard yet that I had to get rid of my bees. These are folks I don't see often, or people I do see regularly but don't have frequent conversations with (like the whole soprano section of the Gwinnett Choral Guild). Every once in a while after rehearsal, one of them will ask, "So, how are your bees getting along, Fran?" And I have to explain the whole rigmarole all over again.

I do wonder when telling that story will cease to feel like such a loss.

The good news is that I'll get to usher Bob (the husband of my main character, Biscuit McKee) through the process of getting bees and learning to deal with them through the next few books in the series.

You can be sure I'm **not** going to write him with an allergy to them.

That shouldn't happen to more than one of us.

BeeAttitude for Day #417: *Blessed are those who eat what is best for them, for they shall glow with good health.*

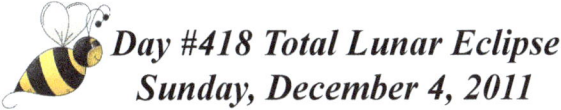 Day #418 Total Lunar Eclipse
Sunday, December 4, 2011

Here I go again, letting you know about interesting goodies from Science.NASA.gov.

If I lived in the western part of the USA, I'd be out at 6:45 a.m. on December 10 to watch a total lunar eclipse. Unfortunately, I live in the Atlanta area, so no eclipse for me. But, I did get to watch a simulation of it that explained why the moon looks bright red during a total lunar eclipse. You wanted to know that, too, didn't you?

Here's the answer: Google NASA Lunar Eclipse (Be sure to click on the triangle to play the video so you can see the simulation.)

Photo Credit: Wikipedia

Don't you love that orange? Here's something else that's orange and wonderful:

BeeAttitude for Day #418: *Blessed are those who step outside and look up, for they shall see wonders untold.*

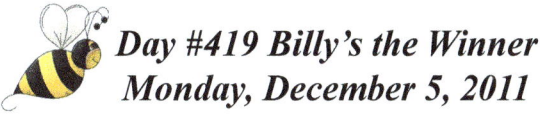 Day #419 Billy's the Winner
Monday, December 5, 2011

I didn't even ask the question, but Billy from Texas answered it.

See if you can beat this one:

Who is a bee's favorite holiday singer?

Cough, cough. Scroll down.

Are you ready?

The envelope, please.

Yep. Billy's the winner, with this answer:

Burl Hives

Just for that, Billy gets to see the bee-yellow cover of the 2nd Biscuit McKee Mystery.

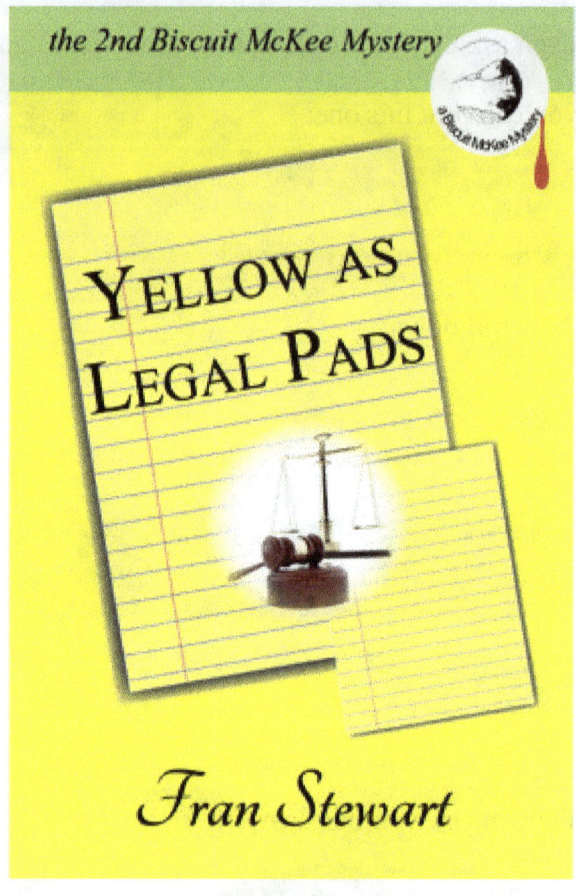

Can you tell I'm going to show one a day for the next few days?

BeeAttitude for Day #419: *Blessed are those who enjoy all the colors, for their days shall be filled with rainbows.*

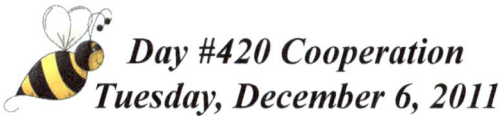 Day #420 Cooperation
Tuesday, December 6, 2011

As I've mentioned many times before, I sing with the Gwinnett Choral Guild. Over the past few weeks we've given three different concerts. The first one was (sort of) a Thanksgiving theme. The second one was all about Christmas. And the one we sang Monday night at Delmar Gardens, a local retirement home, was a combination of the two.

In all three concerts we presented a number of different genres, from classical and baroque to jazz to blues to pop to pure schmaltz – and it was wonderful. I so enjoy singing with a dedicated group of people. We're none of us professionals, but we work together to create some incredible music.

As I was singing my heart out last night, I wondered if bees ever feel the same sort of satisfaction for a job well done. I'd like to think so. Their music certainly resounds as beautifully as ours did.

And here's book #3. Have you noticed yet that the stripe at the top of the book gives the color of the next book in the series?

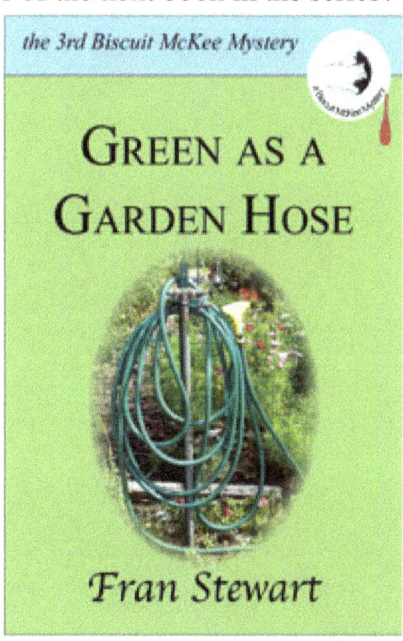

Fran Stewart

BeeAttitude for Day #420: *Blessed are those who buzz beautifully, for they shall spread joy and receive it right back, multiplied.*

BeesKnees #5: A Beekeeping Memoir

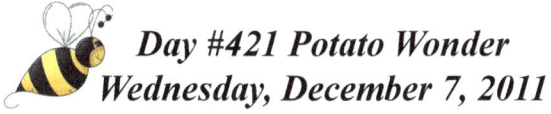
Day #421 Potato Wonder
Wednesday, December 7, 2011

A couple of months ago I harvested my potatoes – the ones I'd grown in the plastic trashcan on my back deck. Remember? I wrote about the experience on Day #345. It started because of a library book. *(See Day #157)*

Well, once I'd dug out all the potatoes, I dumped out the dirt from the can, piled it on top of the compost pile, and forgot about it. I kept adding things to the pile, but didn't turn it all over, the way I was supposed to.

Thank goodness I didn't disturb anything. Went out a couple of weeks ago and found that I must have missed one lonely spud. The darn thing has been growing and is peeking up heartily from the covering of dead leaves. I checked yesterday afternoon and found it's still thriving, despite the iffy weather we've been having.

I'm going to wait until the foliage dies back and then, hopefully, harvest ANOTHER crop of taters. Even if I get only one potato out of it, it'll still be an adventure.

I'll let you know what happens...

And now, here's the cover of the fourth book in the series:

Tomorrow – Indigo

BeeAttitude for Day #421: *Blessed are those who give Mama Nature a chance, for they shall receive happy surprises.*

Day #422 Bees Don't Lose Things
Thursday, December 8, 2011

Bees don't lose things, the way people do. When the Gwinnett Choral Guild had that fund raiser recently, putting together home shows for Premier Jewelry and reaping the benefits because the Jewelry Lady, Judy Parsons, gave a large percentage of her profits to the GCG, I booked two shows.

The way it works is that Premier ships the items to the show hostess (that's Frannie in this case), and the show hostess distributes the goodies to the women who were her guests.

Right.

I had great fun piling the bags in stacks and handing them over to my friends.

Yesterday I was headed out to have lunch with my dear friend Darlene Carter when the phone rang. "Bring my jewelry along when you come," she said.

"Jewelry? Didn't I already give it to you?"

Oh dear. Bees don't have this sort of problem. All they carry around is nectar and pollen. Plus, they clean out cells and dump the garbage outside the hive. That's about it in terms of carrying.

Now, the question is, where did I carry Darlene's bracelet and such? I don't have a beautifully organized hive to search. I've looked in every room in my house, the garage, the car. I've looked under things and in things and on top of things. I'm pretty sure those silver-colored Premier boxes are … somewhere … I think …

Fortunately, Darlene is quite forgiving. She was nice enough to say, "Maybe you did deliver them, and I just misplaced them."

Ha!

She may be forgiving, but I still have to find those blinkin' things. Either that or order another set for her. Wish me luck, will you?

And here's the picture of Indigo's cover, as I promised. If you haven't read this one yet, don't read the next one (VIOLET) until after you've finished INDIGO. I leave some loose threads at the end of INDIGO that don't get answered for a while. And, anyway, if you read VIOLET first, you'll find out who gets killed in INDIGO. It would be a shame to spoil the suspense.

BeeAttitude for Day #422: *Blessed are those who know where they're flying, for they shall find their way out and back again.*

Day #423 Ancestry
Friday, December 9, 2011

Bee's ancestors looked the same as bees look today. Scientists found a honeybee embedded in amber 140 million years old, and it was recognizable as a honeybee.

The rest of us, though, haven't been around in our current form for nearly that long. Here's proof:

Sorry - I couldn't resist it ...

This came from Dave Coverly's website at speedbump.com

BeeAttitude for Day #423: *Blessed are those who are aware of where they came from, for they shall have a better chance of figuring out where they're going.*

Fran Stewart

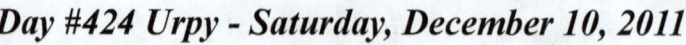 Day #424 Urpy - Saturday, December 10, 2011

I was pouring myself a cup of tea a few minutes ago as I looked out at the deck where the beehives used to be. My white teapot has a thin blue ring around the top and a ladybug drip-stopper on the spout.

Other than the ladybug, my teapot is quite ordinary. It reminds me of the empty-looking deck.

I'd rather have bees there.

And a teapot that looks like this:

BeeAttitude for Day #424: *Blessed are those who drink water, for they shall be healthy indeed.*

p.s. from Fran: "Urpy" the rooster teapot—which is really a pitcher—lives with the **Grads to Grans Book Club.** They also have a "teapot" that looks like a frog. It makes a "riddip" sound when milk or juice pours from its mouth/spout! Take a look:

Day #425 The Second Crop Went Bust
Sunday, December 11, 2011

Here I thought I might get a second crop of potatoes. I knew they'd probably be pretty small, but I thought there just might be a possibility.

Unh-unh. The weather turned too cold for this perky little plant to make it. Its feet were in the compost pile. All it needed to do was grow really fast.

I should have known better.

Now it looks like this:

I know I kill off lots of characters in my mysteries without blinking an eye. You'd think I could be blasé about the death of this hopeful little potato that grew in my compost pile just before winter set in.

Queen bees stop laying eggs before the weather gets too cold, and the bees that emerge from the cells in the fall are more attuned to winter survival than the summertime bees are.

Too bad potatoes never learned that lesson.

BeeAttitude for Day #425: *Blessed are those who live attuned to the seasons, for they shall have fewer disappointments.*

Day #426 Another Speed Bump
Monday, December 12, 2011

I know this blog is supposed to be about bees, but every once in a while (and more often lately it seems) I just have to include another jewel from Dave Coverly's website at speedbump.com.

© 2010 Dave *Coverly*

I'll be back to the bees tomorrow.

BeeAttitude for Day #426: *Blessed are those who are flexible, for they shall not get bent out of shape.*

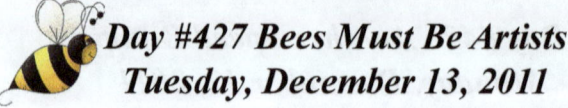 Day #427 Bees Must Be Artists
Tuesday, December 13, 2011

I was thinking about people who live—and work—well into their nineties. Most of those people, at least the ones I know about, are highly creative. Artists, musicians, writers just don't seem to retire. They keep on creating. Pablo Cassals, Grandma Moses, Artur Rubenstein, and Lillian Jackson Braun come to mind.

Bees are like that, too. They work until the end of their life span. They generally die while they're still working, trying to get just one more load of pollen and nectar back to the hive. When their little wings wear out, they simply can't go on.

One woman, though, who has been an inspiration to a number of generations, worked and worked and stopped before her wings wore out. She's the well-known Georgia pediatrician, Dr. Leila Denmark. You may have heard of her. She's 113 years old now. *[**2019 Note**: Dr. Denmark died at the age of 114 (and 60 days) on April 1, 2012.]*

BeesKnees #5: A Beekeeping Memoir

(photo credit, from an online article written for the National Library of Medicine, titled Changing the Face of Medicine: Celebrating America's Physicians*)*

Dr. Denmark retired (sort of) when she was 103, only because her eyesight had gotten too poor for her to feel completely confident of her diagnoses. Due to macular degeneration, she is now legally blind. But I've heard that she'll still take calls from her former patients and give out good advice.

One thing I find wonderful is that she's known for her own work, rather than just for the fact that she's lived more than a century.

We should all be so lucky.

Finding work to do that we love (and that we're willing to devote our lives to) is a rather old-fashioned concept. Many people now change their jobs almost as often as they change their underwear. Yuck! Hope that's not true.

What a role model! Between Dr. Denmark and the bees, I have a lot to live up to.

And a long time left to do it.

Next to her, I'm just a spring chicken.

BeeAttitude for Day #427: *Blessed are those who love the work they do, for they shall play every day.*

Day #428 Allergies? Don't Worry!
Wednesday, December 14, 2011

Tuesday night the Gwinnett County Beekeepers listened to master beekeeper B.J. Weeks tell about his experiences running 500 hives in one season. Whew! Wouldn't want to work the 40-hour days he works during a honey flow. That's right. That's what I said. A **40-hour day**, meaning you get going and you don't stop until the work is done.

He said one thing that floored most of us, though. He asked us why people should eat local honey if they're trying to alleviate allergies. We gave the standard and well-accepted answer that beekeepers have been preaching for ages. Heck, I've even talked about it here in this blog. Pollen/honey made from local plants acts on the allergies that develop from that same pollen.

Nonsense (according to BJ Weeks). Local honey from ANYWHERE will help alleviate allergies. You could eat local honey from California, even though you live in Georgia, and it would still help you. The reason? It has nothing to do with where the honey comes from or what pollen was used in making it. Local honey is not highly processed. THAT'S where the value comes in. Heating and heavy filtering of honey is what takes out the beneficial aspects of the honey. Small local beekeepers don't do all that stuff to their honey, so you get all the benefits.

Now, for another reason why it doesn't matter if your "local" honey came from halfway across the continent—honeybees gather the **heavy pollen** that stays in the plants (until the bees remove it). Allergies are caused by types of **air-born pollen** that are much lighter than the ones the bees gather.

That makes sense. It goes against everything I've been preaching, but it does make sense.

So, from now on, when someone sends me honey from Arizona (thank you, Ellen), or Hawaii (thank you again, Ellen!), or Michigan (thank you, Donna), or Oregon (thank you, Marta), or Greece (thank you, Veronica), I will not only eat it with gusto, I will also be able to say, "Look how good this is for me!" at the same time.

BeeAttitude for Day #428: *Blessed are those who are willing to unlearn and learn anew, for they shall be constantly surprised.*

Day #429 BeesKnees Bee Report!
Thursday, December 15, 2011

Tuesday evening at the Gwinnett Beekeepers meeting, I asked Rob Alexander how my bees were doing. You'll remember that he took both hives to Rancho Alegre after I developed the allergy to bee stings. *[2019 Note: It's now known as Alegre Farm]*

Turns out that the bees in one of the hives are as gentle as sunrise over a tree-lined meadow. The other hive, though—and don't ask me what the difference is because I haven't a clue—turned out to be what beekeepers call peppery. That mean they're cranky as all get-out. But that peppery hive is the one that's absolutely LOADED with honey.

Now, since both beehives came from the same bee farm, and since I treated them both pretty much the same, what could make two hives be so opposite in nature? It's probably the queen's genetics. Other than that, who knows?

Rob's pretty sure that the peppery hive [that sounds so much better than "the mean hive," doesn't it?] is going to produce lots of honey come the spring honey flow.

Let's hope he's right.

BeeAttitude for Day #429: *Blessed are those who share their enthusiasms, for they shall spread joy and have it bounce back into their lives.*

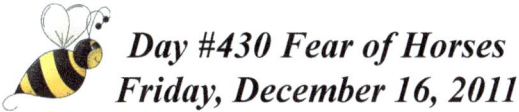 Day #430 Fear of Horses
Friday, December 16, 2011

Ever since I was a little girl, I've been afraid of horses. They're pretty big, and I worry that they might step on me. Or bite me.

But, just as I learned that around bees I simply need to take precautions and I'll be safe, I think it's time for me to learn the same thing around horses. I know a woman, a psychotherapist, who does incredible therapeutic work using horses as – well, strange as it sounds – as co-therapists.

I'm going to check it out. It may take me until the spring to get my nerve up, but right now I'm making a public commitment that I WILL make an appointment with her. I WILL tackle this fear of mine. And I WILL overcome it.

Hold me to it, will you?

BeeAttitude for Day #430: *Blessed are those who plant window boxes, for we shall pollinate their flowers with joyous abandon.*

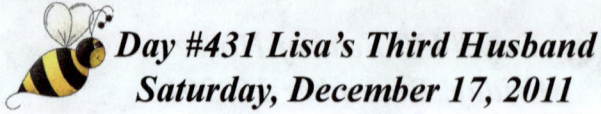 Day #431 Lisa's Third Husband
Saturday, December 17, 2011

I was walking down the Audiobook section of my favorite Gwinnett County Library branch, and found *Why My Third Husband Will Be a Dog*, written and recorded by Lisa Scottoline. It's a series of essays about life in general, specifically about her life as a woman who's been divorced twice.

It got me to thinking. Maybe I could record all these blog posts and put them up on Audible.com. I'm not quite sure about how to do it, but I do have a good microphone, and I have several friends who could probably rescue me if I get totally mired in unfamiliar technology.

The only trouble is – what will I do about all the pictures I've used?

Do I describe them:

"Here's a red flower."

"Here's a blue flower with a bee on it."

"You'll have to imagine this picture from Day #363 (October 10th) of Aggie Pete being hugged by Clutch, the great big Houston Rockets mascot."

Do I ignore the pictures?

I suppose I could, but how will that work when I have a picture that's an integral part of a particular post? How would I handle the post about my grandchildren throwing the thistle seeds up into the sunbeams streaming through the skylights?

Do I work out some sort of compromise between the two systems?

Somehow I'm not sure an audio book like that will fly, but I'd really like to try it. When my bees went to a new home, they didn't curl up in their hive and say, "We don't know the flowers in this area." No! They ventured forth into unknown territory and filled their hive with honey.

So, should I venture out?

What do you think? Any ideas? Should I do it?

And how?

BeeAttitude for Day #431: *Blessed are those who put themselves on the line for something they believe in, the way we foraging bees do every time we leave the hive, for they shall rest easy, knowing their lives are fulfilled.*

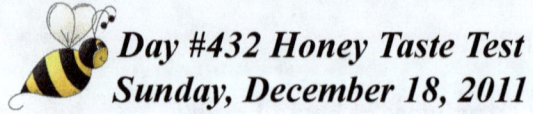

Day #432 Honey Taste Test
Sunday, December 18, 2011

I've been eating comb honey from north Georgia for the past few months, ever since the Gwinnett County Fair, where I bought several jars of Sourwood Honey. I love its buttery, almost nutty taste and its shimmery golden color.

But a few days ago, I went to the December meeting of the National League of American Pen Women. The women in our Atlanta Branch are great fun. I thoroughly enjoy meeting monthly with such highly creative, vital women. As I was leaving, after the meeting, Sally Hodges handed me a jar of honey. I tried to upload a picture of it, but for some reason I can't get it to load, so you'll just have to imagine the luscious, dark, rich, chocolate-y color. I have no idea what kind of honey it is, but the taste reminds me of maple syrup.

During the twenty-six years I lived in Vermont, I tried all the different grades of maple syrup and decided that the very best one for me was what they used to call Grade C. The C stood for commercial. It was the darkest, richest syrup you can imagine.

Then political correctness and marketing mania invaded the Green Mountain State, and Grade A became Grade AAA. Grade B was called Grade AA. And good ole Grade C became Grade A. The assumption, I think, was that people would think Grade C was sub-standard. This is the same sort of thought pattern that had people trying to change the town of Hog Mountain, GA, into Hamilton Mill. The ludicrous knows no geographic boundaries.

So, now, here I sit with a whole jar full—well, almost full; I already ate a bunch—of the richest darkest yummiest honey I've tasted in a long time.

Call it **Grade C Honey**.

That's the highest compliment I can give it.

BeeAttitude for Day #432: *Blessed are those who read (especially those who read about us bees!), for they shall live in a limitless world.*

Fran Stewart

Day #433 Bleak House
Monday, December 19, 2011

I generally read four books at a time. One is the red room book. Just so you'll know what I'm talking about, I name the rooms in my house by the color of the floor. The red room book is the one I go to when I have a few minutes (or a bunch of minutes), usually in the evening, but occasionally as I'm munching lunch. My red room book today is *The China Conspiracy*, a suspense-thriller by p.m. terrell. (This is not a typo. It's the way her name appears on her books, without capitalization.) I interviewed p.m. terrell on the radio show I hosted in 2009. At the time I read all her books (so I could conduct an intelligent one-hour interview), and it's time to re-read them. I do that with books I truly enjoy.

My green room book was *The Eighty Dollar Champion* by Elizabeth Letts. I say my green room book *was*, because I finished it last night, crying through the last chapter. It's the story of Snowman, the plow horse who was on his way to the slaughterhouse when he was bought by a man who taught at a riding school. Turns out the horse was a natural jumper – who then went on to win the 1958 National Horse Show and who inspired a nation.

My blue room book is the one I blogged about last Saturday. The blue room book is usually an audio book, and I play it while I'm cooking, washing dishes (yes—washing them. The only dishwasher in this house isn't a machine), knitting, or doing Killer Sudoku. Yes, I can multi-task.

But the book I'd really like to mention today is *Bleak House* by Charles Dickens. I've spent lots of years discounting Dickens. All he did, so most people think, was write lots of words – he was, or so we've all heard, paid by the word. Lots of description, lots of repetition. Yeah, yeah, yeah. I read *A Christmas Carol* years ago, but I'd rather watch George C. Scott as Scrooge.

But something changed my mind. Months ago, I heard a casual reference (by a total stranger) to *Nicholas Nickleby*. I read it and enjoyed it. So I'm on a streak, here. I decided to read through Dickens. So far, my favorite by far is *Bleak House*. It's my car book. Audio book, that is. *Bleak House* is not a casual read by any means, even if it's someone else doing the reading and I'm only doing the listening. There are 31 CDs in this set. THIRTY-ONE!!! I've had to renew it twice, which is the limit for renewals at the Gwinnett County Library.

It's worth it, though. All those wonderful hours of listening—and the actor reading it, David Case, has a repertoire of voices that is astonishing.

I'd like to quote one little sentence, just to give you a taste. Dickens was describing **a man whose "mouth was overstuffed with teeth, rather like a pianoforte with too many keys."** Don't you just love it?

Now, what does my reading list – or this vivid description – have to do with bees? Nothing, I guess. It's just that on a cold December evening, I get to read, while bees have to cluster, keeping themselves warm.

On a long drive, I get to listen to the words of great writers. On a long journey to or from a nectar source, bees listen to the wind, or so I suppose.

As I walk from room to room in my house, a book I'm actively reading graces each of them, and I can stop to enjoy each one. When bees walk from comb to comb in their hive, they have to do the one job that is theirs to do, whether it be to feed the larvae, clean the cells, fan the nectar to evaporate the moisture, or guard the hive. They don't get a choice.

Poor bees. Lucky me.

BeeAttitude for Day #433: *Blessed are those who love what they do, for they shall fly through life with a joyful purpose.*

Fran Stewart

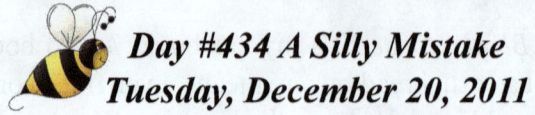
Day #434 A Silly Mistake
Tuesday, December 20, 2011

Last April, ten days after my bees arrived, I decided to keep a log of what appeared to be their reactions to the weather. I wasn't very consistent with it. In fact, after a while I forgot all about it.

But I pulled up the document this morning, thinking it was something else. What an eye-opener. My very first entry was this:

4/27/11:

Tornados/hail predicted.

Morning clear. Bees normal.

4:15 pm Cloudy. Wind picked up. Countless bees swirling around entrance hole and hive, as if every forager wanted to get back inside at the same time. Both hives exhibited this behavior.

Bad thunderstorms and wind after midnight. No storm activity in afternoon, though.

When I read it, I saw right away what had happened. On April 27, I'd seen a hatch-out. I was a beginning beekeeper, though, and I didn't know a hatch-out when I saw one—which is why I mistook their activity for a weather-related event. There had obviously been a disturbance in the hive more than three weeks before that day, some event that temporarily stopped the queen from laying. Then, 21 days before all that activity I saw, the queen had resumed her egg laying. You might remember that it takes 21 days for a bee to go from egg to hatching. If you don't remember, check back to Day #209. I wrote about the hatch-out and what I'd learned from it on Day #332.

I thought about it, and remembered that there had been evidence of tornado damage when I drove to South Georgia to pick up my bees on April 17th. In fact, a tornado had ripped out part of the bee yard, and the folks there were still rebuilding the shed where they constructed their hives.

So this morning I Googled **"georgia tornado march 2011"** and found that a series of tornados had ripped through the state between the 18th and the 27th of March. I'm guessing, of course, but it seems logical that a tornado passing by a hive would be ample reason for a queen to shut down, at least temporarily. She must have felt more secure, though, by April 6th, in order to lay the batch of eggs that all hatched on the 27th and sent me into a flurry of concern.

I hadn't seen any such activity in the 10 days I'd had the hives on my back deck, simply because there weren't any babies ready to hatch yet.

Just goes to show you, there's always something new to learn.

BeeAttitude for Day #434: *Blessed are those who pay attention to the world around them, for they shall see amazing sights.*

bee.s. from Fran – blessed are those who pore over old documents, for they shall be pleasantly surprised.

another bee.s. – blessed are those who journal, for they (and those who come after them) shall have a record of their days.

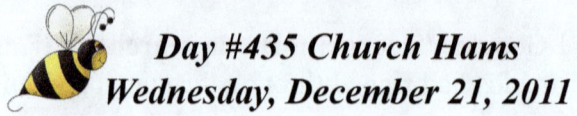

Day #435 Church Hams
Wednesday, December 21, 2011

Don't ever plan a book signing on a day when a local megachurch is giving away 5,000 hams. Last Saturday a local church – one of those that has a sanctuary that looks like a football stadium and holds almost as many people – booked the local ballpark for a giveaway event. Drive through, open your trunk, and church volunteers will put a Honey Baked Ham in there.

It sounded like a very good idea. Even I, with no TV, heard about it, because I saw an article placed prominently in the paper. And I was glad that families who couldn't afford a big holiday meal would, like Bob Crachit's family, delight in a feast.

The trouble, though, was that my local bookstore was holding an Author Gala that day, from 1:00 to 4:00, with eight local authors signing books, a band providing music, and lots of goodies to eat.

The roads were so jammed for five or more MILES around the stadium, nobody could get to the store. The band never made it. One author showed up three hours late, and another one got there only because her husband drove her in their golf cart along the sidewalks! For the first hour and a half of the signing event, we authors were the only ones in the store besides the staff. The good news is that we all had lots of goodies to eat.

Interstate 85 was, I heard, at a standstill for 15 miles south of the exit.

That's ridiculous. I'm very happy that the church leaders wanted to be so generous. But whatever happened to the right hand not knowing what the left hand was doing? Isn't that the way charity is supposed to work?

Local businesses were badly hurt by the fact that for an entire day people simply couldn't reach them. People waiting in line with their engines running for two, three, or even four hours, probably spent more on gas than they would have spent if they'd bought their own ham. And several people who did make it into the store told us that there were more luxury cars in the ham-line than there were the old clunkers you'd expect people to be driving if they were truly needy.

So, next year (when the church has said they're going to give away **10,000** hams, since this event was so successful), I wish they'd quietly give those hams to other churches, to the Salvation Army, to the various food banks around the Metro area, and let them distribute to those who truly need the food.

And let the bookstores have their customers.

BeeAttitude for Day #435: *Blessed are those who refrain from robbing the hives of other bees, for their consciences shall be clear.*

bee.s. from Fran: Today is the first day of the last year on the Mayan Calendar. Just thought you'd like to know.

Happy Solstice!

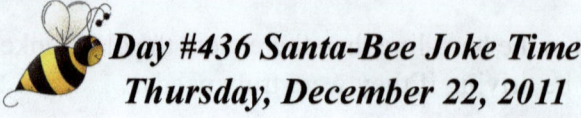

Day #436 Santa-Bee Joke Time
Thursday, December 22, 2011

What do you get when you cross a **honeybee** with **Santa Claus**?

It's that time of year!

Send me your answers and we'll see who wins...

BeeAttitude for Day #436: *Blessed are those who laugh hard every day, for their tummies shall work well.*

 ### Day #437 Biscuit and Panther
Friday, December 23, 2011

December 25th will be eight years since Biscuit, my very first cat, died. And today, the 23rd, I'm missing Panther, who died in my arms this day in 2008.

Biscuit on my shoulder (2002)

Panther

I promise not to mention my late cats on Christmas day, but I just wanted to get this yearly December sadness out of my system before then.

Thank you for letting me cry on your (virtual) shoulder.

BeeAttitude for Day #437: *Blessed are those who mourn for those they loved, for their tears shall wash away their sadness.*

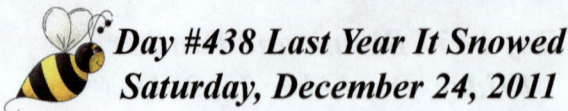Day #438 Last Year It Snowed
Saturday, December 24, 2011

In 2010 it snowed in Georgia on Christmas Day. The bees didn't mind, I suppose, although I didn't have my bees yet. They just hunkered down a little closer in their clusters and kept themselves warm by vibrating their unhinged flight muscles and walking slowly toward the center of the cluster and then back out again. I know they did, because that's what bees do in cold weather.

It's a lovely system that's kept the bees in good stead for hundreds of millions of years.

This year, they'll probably be out looking for pollen (and not finding much). It's supposed to be in the 60s on Christmas Day. As I write this, it's raining, so all I can wish is –

♪ May your days be merry and bright,

and may all your Christmases be dry. ♪

Somehow that doesn't quite ring the right way, does it? Bing Crosby would be horrified.

BeeAttitude for Day #438: *Blessed are those who sing anyway, for they shall keep themselves company.*

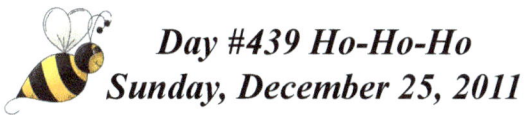 ***Day #439 Ho-Ho-Ho***
Sunday, December 25, 2011

Radar is the true Spirit of Christmas.

Radar

Ho-ho-ho! Now you know!

BeeAttitude for Day #439: *Blessed are those who give of themselves, for they shall leave happy footprints in time.*

Day #440 Night Sight - Moon, Venus, Jupiter
Monday, December 26, 2011

All you have to do this evening to see an amazing sight is to walk outside after sunset and look to the west.

The moon, with earthshine illuminating the vast bulk of it, will be joined by Venus and Jupiter in one of those spectacular shows that most of us miss – first because they're not a daily occurrence, and secondly because most of us don't look up at the night sky.

Photo Credit: A Venus-Moon conjunction photographed in Nov. 2011 by Thad V'Soske of Fruita, CO. Copyright: T. V'Soske/Cosmotions.com

If you read the story in NASA Science News, you'll learn what the Da Vinci Glow is.

Enjoy the sight!

BeeAttitude for Day #440: *Blessed are those who look up in wonder, for they shall see miracles.*

Day #441 A December 26th Tradition
Tuesday, December 27, 2011

Every year, on the day after Christmas, I sit down and hand-write my thank-you letters. With a pen. On paper. On the 27th, I put them in the mail.

Yes. Snail Mail. With a stamp.

I have a friend on the West coast who hasn't written a letter in five years – or so she told me in an email. "Email is so much faster," she said (that is, she typed). Nancy is trying to talk me into tweeting, but I've remained a dinosaur where that is concerned.

Who says that every communication has to be instantaneous? It seems the whole world is beginning to think that way. Instant everything. Books (like *Bleak House* that I blogged about on Day #433) used to be doled out in monthly installments, giving people a chance to talk about the latest chapter for four weeks before the next one came out. Letters from the Old Country used to take months to get to the colonies (if they made it at all what with the dangers of sailing across the Atlantic). Letters were written to be worth reading at the other end, because the writer knew that the reader would treasure the words, unfold and refold the paper, hold it and feel a connection, however tenuous, across the miles.

Nowadays, it's the tweet. What, I ask you, is worth treasuring there?

Bees need instantaneous communication. When a queen dies, the entire colony must know about it within moments. They have to get busy creating a new queen. Their survival depends on it.

But whose survival, may I ask, depends on knowing what Person A ate for breakfast?

My friend (and I told her I was going to blog about this) sends Christmas cards, with a one-page (both sides) summary of everything she and her family have done all year – the kids, the grandkids, the vacations, the business trips. Each year, before I read it, I always skip to the end to see if she penned a personal note to me. (She never does, but I keep hoping.) "Dear Friends" her letter begins, and I know I'm pretty far down on the list, with a last name that starts with S.

Want to bet I get a letter from her after she reads this blog?

BeeAttitude for Day #441: *Blessed are those who tell what needs to be told, for they shall keep the hive healthy.*

bee.s. from Fran – love ya, Nancy! Write me!

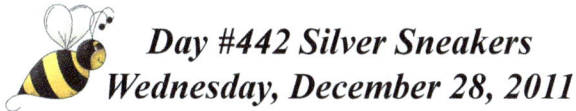 Day #442 Silver Sneakers
Wednesday, December 28, 2011

Bees don't need an exercise program. They work hard all their life long. Once they start flying out to forage, they simply don't stop except at night. They must be in great shape. Unlike me.

But now I find that there's an exercise program for us old farts – it's called Silver Sneakers, and I'm going to try it out next month.

Today I visited a gym up the road a ways. I've never been in a fitness center in my whole life. I'm not against exercise, it's just that I could never figure out why somebody would pay to go to an exercise place when they could just walk around the neighborhood three or four times a week.

Right.

The trouble is, I haven't been walking around my neighborhood even once a week. There are some big noisy scary dogs who get out of their yards periodically. I don't want to take the risk.

There aren't any dogs at the fitness center.

There's a sauna, though. And a dance-exercise class (an easy one designed for people who have trouble running upstairs).

I'm starting next week. I'll let you know how it turns out.

BeeAttitude for Day #442: *Blessed are those who dance through life, for they shall have healthy hearts.*

Day #443 Be a Bee in the Sistine Chapel
Thursday, December 29, 2011

Wouldn't it be fun to be able to fly like a bee? Well – there's a really cool website that makes it possible for you to fly around the Sistine Chapel exactly the way a bee could, zooming in on all the bright and beautiful colors. I'm sure a bee would be confused by them, since there are so many lovely flower-shades.

Here's the site: http://www.vatican.va/various/cappelle/sistina_vr/index.html

Just move your mouse the direction you want to fly—uh—I mean look.

Enjoy.

BeeAttitude for Day #443: *Blessed are those who share the wonder, for they shall find even <u>more</u> wonder.*

bee.s. from Fran: Thanks to my friend, artist Mikki Root Dillon, who sent me the link.

Day #444 The Penultimate Day of the Year
Friday, December 30, 2011

Penultimate. Don't you love that word?

The first time I ever heard it was on public radio years and years ago. I think the announcer was talking about the penultimate day of a month, but maybe I was listening on December 30th of that particular year.

This morning I got to wondering where the word came from, so, of course, I looked it up. It's a word from the late seventeenth century. Somebody—don't you wonder who?—came up with this variation of the Latin word paenultimus, which is a combination of paene, which means *almost*, and ultimus, which means *last*.

So, on this penultimate day of 2011—almost the last day of the year—the bees and I wish you a lovely ending to this year and a glorious beginning to the next one.

BeeAttitude for Day #444: *Blessed are those who delight in the sounds of buzzing, for they shall have their ears filled with glory.*

Fran Stewart

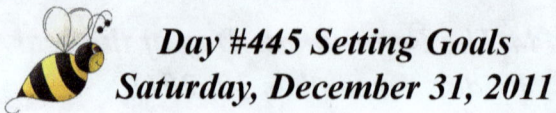

Day #445 Setting Goals
Saturday, December 31, 2011

I've never been one for New Year's Resolutions. When I wrote a column for the Atlanta Writer's Club EQuill, I came up with resolutions (all related to writing, of course), but for the most part, resolutions and I just don't get along.

Years ago I went to a therapist who ran me through an exercise in which I was to describe various subjects she suggested – a field, a stream, a valley, some mountains, a cave, and so on. Each of these, she told me afterwards, was supposed to represent some aspect of my life. When she asked me to describe the mountains (which, she told me later, supposedly represented the goals in my life), I couldn't see any. I knew there were mountains there, far away, but they were covered with clouds all the way down to their base.

Doesn't say much about me as a long-range planner, does it?

When I wrote my first book, I had no idea it would turn into a series. When I first decided to keep bees, I didn't think much farther than a hazy (cloud-covered) notion of getting honey some day and saving the environment in the meantime. Instead, I just enjoyed the process of planning for them, of writing this blog, of installing them on my deck. I simply enjoyed the process each and every day.

For 2012, though, I've decided to set some goals – sort of. I'm going to go visit friends I haven't seen in quite a while. I'm going:

- to Florida to see Karen & Dan,

- to Lumberton to see Trish,

- to Vermont to see Shar & Greg, and

- to the Raleigh area to see Annie.

I'll be busy in 2012.

If you want to visit me this coming year, be sure you call first! There's no telling where I'll BEE.

BeeAttitude for Day #445: *Blessed are those who stay in touch with old flowers, for they shall find welcoming nectar at the end of their flight.*

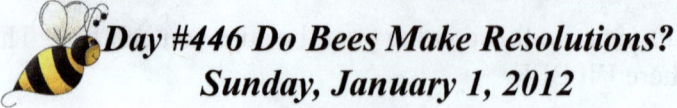Day #446 Do Bees Make Resolutions?
Sunday, January 1, 2012

A Bee's Weekly Resolutions for the New Year:

I will do my job, every day, all day long.

I will do my job, every day, all day.

I will do my job, every day.

I will do my job.

I will do.

I will.

Six exhausting weeks. That's the length of a worker bee's life.

Bless their little hearts.

Happy New Year.

BeeAttitude for Day #446: *Blessed are those who do the work they are intended for, for they shall brighten the world around them.*

Day #447 How Do Bees Measure?
Monday, January 2, 2012

I was listening this morning to an audio book set in old England, and one of the characters referred to twelve shillings being worth 144 pence. So now I know that it took 12 pennies to make a shilling.

Years ago, when Canada was shifting from the old measurements of feet and inches to the metric system, there was a Canadian television commercial that featured a gorgeous woman flouting her measurements. "I'm 91-61-91," she would say breathlessly, and few people who saw that commercial ever forgot what the metric equivalent of 36-24-36 was. Actually, 36 inches is 91.44 centimeters, and 24 inches is 60.96 centimeters. But 91-61-91 was close enough for all of us to get the idea.

So, aside from the fact that America is in the dark ages where measurements are concerned – but I won't step onto that soapbox – what sort of measurements would honeybees use?

This is one I came up with:

Give 'em a wing, and they'll take a meadow-width.

Can you think of any others?

BeeAttitude for Day #447: *Blessed are those who faithfully feed their hive, no matter how many meadows they have to fly across, for they shall find sustenance themselves in plenty.*

Day #448 Silver Sneakers Report
Tuesday, January 3, 2012

Well, I did it. I went to BodyPlex yesterday and swiped my Silver Sneakers card.

Then I looked around at all those machines – and headed for the cycle room. I know how to do that without accidentally pulling the wrong muscle. I haven't ridden on a bicycle since I wrecked my bike in fourth grade by slamming it into a brick wall. Not intentionally. There was a spread of gravel on the pavement, and when I tried to turn to the left, the gravel helped my front wheel slip out, straight ahead. Where the wall was.

I limped home, dragging my twisted bike along with me, and never got another bike throughout my childhood. *You break it, you do without it* was the philosophy in my family.

Still, yesterday I thought I couldn't go wrong on a stationary bike. They keep the lights low in that room—apparently so nobody can see what anyone else is doing during the classes. I didn't have to worry, though. I was the only person in there.

I looked at the clock, climbed on, slipped my feet into the stirrups, and started to pedal. I made it for ten minutes before my legs were completely jelly. Fortunately I didn't collapse when I stepped off the machine.

I made an appointment for a one-hour orientation so I can use the other machines.

And then I went and sat in the sauna for a while. Ahhhh! Love that exercise!

BeeAttitude for Day #448: *Blessed are those who move with joy, for they shall fly happily throughout life.*

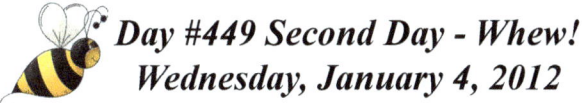 *Day #449 Second Day - Whew!*
Wednesday, January 4, 2012

I made it through my second day at the gym—and my first Silver Sneakers Class. The other members of the class were very welcoming – and we started the class by singing Happy Birthday to a member who turned 89 on New Year's Day. I figured I could easily keep up.

Ha!

By halfway through the class I was doing five repetitions for every 8 the instructor counted out. Thank goodness the last exercises were done sitting in a chair!

Then I went out to the treadmills. The woman on a machine across the aisle was reading a book while she walked. I'll have to remember to take a book next time. I walked for 15 minutes while I waited for my 1:00 appointment with the Personal Training Manager.

At 1:00 the manager told me I was in no shape to consider a personal training program. He wasn't quite that blunt, of course. He diplomatically asked me how I'd enjoyed the Silver Sneakers Class, and when I told him how out of breath I'd gotten, he said I still had a lot of work to do and ought to wait a few months before even considering a trainer.

Suited me just fine. I have to get to where I can keep up with an 89-year-old!

BeeAttitude for Day #449: *Blessed are those who do what they can with what they have, for they shall eventually create honey.*

Day #450 What's the Diagnosis Code?
Thursday, January 5, 2012

It's time to admit that I just turned 65. Yesterday I went to the Hope Clinic in Lawrenceville for my "Welcome to Medicare Physical." Several people I've talked to since then said, "So it was free, huh?"

"Nope," I said. "I paid for it over the years, and now I'm reaping the benefit."

Anyway, this physical, something bees never have to go through, is designed to establish a base line for any future exams. After the doctor asked, discussed, prodded, measured, and poked, he glanced at his paperwork, looked confused, and said, "Uh...um...excuse me a moment, please," and he left the room.

When he came back some time later he told me that he'd "had no idea what was the diagnosis code for perfectly healthy," since he hardly ever used it, so he'd had to go ask someone.

He also told me that if I didn't want a colonoscopy, he didn't see any reason why I had to have one.

He's my kind of doctor!

BeeAttitude for Day #450: *Blessed are those who do what they have to do when they have to do it, for they shall feel a good sense of accomplishment.*

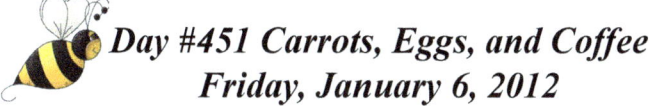 Day #451 Carrots, Eggs, and Coffee
Friday, January 6, 2012

Here's another blog post that has nothing to do with bees.

A friend of mine in Australia shared an interesting story with me recently about a wise old woman who helped a younger woman deal with adversity. "Dig up some carrots," she said, "and gather some eggs, then bring me some ground coffee beans."

She did as directed, and then was instructed to put them all in boiling water. So she took three pots, brought water to boil, and put the carrots in one, the eggs in another, and the coffee in the third.

"Look at them," the older woman said after a while. "What do you see?"

The young woman replied, "They've all cooked."

"Yes," said the wise woman, "but look at the differences. The **carrots** were hard and resistant when they were put in the water, but they softened up and gave in to the heat. The **eggs**, with their soft vulnerability, became hard in the boiling water. As for the **coffee**? Well, it changed the water!

We all have adversity. But how each one of us reacts to that adversity is up to us. Will we be carrots, eggs, or coffee?

BeeAttitude for Day #451: *Blessed are those who cook with joy no matter what they cook, for they shall spread happiness.*

Fran Stewart

Day #452 Best Bees in the Yard
Saturday, January 7, 2012

A few nights ago the Board of the Gwinnett County Beekeepers Club met, discussed business, and then devolved into a general discussion of how our various bees were doing. There were, alas, some sad stories. One woman had lost both her hives; one man had lost about 50% of his numerous hives.

The funny thing was that nobody knows why some beehives die and other hives survive. Oh, there are a kazillion theories out there—about as many theories as there are beekeepers. But don't ever believe anyone who says he knows absolutely which beekeeping practices will allow hives to survive.

I got more and more worried, particularly when Rob Alexander, the man who is keeping my hives, said he'd had trouble with his. He wasn't sure his hives were going to survive till Spring.

"Rob," I said with a great deal of trepidation, "what about my hives? How are they doing?"

"You're hives are the healthiest ones in my bee yard," he said. "They're mean as the dickens, but they sure are strong."

He told us how he had taken the frames out of each of my hives and placed five of my frames in a ten-frame box, filled the box with additional empty frames, then did the same with the next five frames.

Within two weeks, he said, the bees were overflowing those boxes, so he put on an additional layer, and now they've filled those layers as well.

"Why are they doing so well?" I asked.

"I think it's because you hardly ever worked them," he said. Beekeepers who are anxious to learn about their hives generally make a habit of opening the hives once a week—or more often—to inspect them. I never did that, particularly once I started having bad reactions to the stings. I just let them do their thing.

BeesKnees #5: A Beekeeping Memoir

Think about it. That's the way bees live in the wild. Unless there's a visit from a marauding bear, wild hives are seldom opened to the outside air and light.

So, just think of me as a venerable hollow oak tree, sheltering my bees for the time I had them here. But then again, that's just one of MANY theories.

BeeAttitude for Day #452: *Blessed are those who let well enough alone, for they shall encourage and benefit from natural growth.*

bee.s. from Fran: I rather like the idea of being an oak tree.

Day #453 Butter, Butter, Butter
Sunday, January 8, 2012

I bought a gallon of fresh cow's milk recently—milk that hadn't been homogenized, so by the time I woke up the next morning, there was a thick layer of cream on the top. I poured it off into a canning jar, screwed on the lid, and started shaking. Ten or fifteen minutes later, I drained off the leftover (now creamless) milk, and had myself a good-sized yellow lump of sheer heaven. I poured the milk over my morning oatmeal.

There's just nothing in the world like truly fresh butter. The author of *Eat Right for Your Type* says that my O-positive blood type is not supposed to eat dairy products, with the one exception of Mozzarella Cheese. Butter is considered neutral for O+, so I figure I can continue to eat it without guilt.

Especially if I mix it with honey.

Just like a lot of people where religion is concerned, I'm going to pay attention to the strictures I agree with and let the others slide. I love Mozzarella, so the author must know what's right for me. Yogurt is a special favorite of mine, though, so that author really doesn't know anything, right? Cheddar, Pepperjack, Brie, Parmesano-Reggiano, all the dozens of other cheeses I adore?

I've decided to ignore that book.

BeeAttitude for Day #453: *Blessed are those who enjoy every bite they eat (especially the honey!), for their food shall nourish them well.*

Day #454 Honeybee Sanctuary
Monday, January 9, 2012

I just saw a website for a honeybee sanctuary in Florida. It's called Spikenard Farm, and the background picture on their home page makes me drool. All that lush green and the gorgeous bee-friendly flowers!

I'm going to quote them directly from the Sanctuary tab on their site (I'm the one who bolded several of the phrases):

Spikenard Farm Honeybee Sanctuary was founded in **the certainty that there can be a better future for the honeybees.** Today the sanctuary has become more and more an **oasis of beauty, peace, and joy.**

The Spikenard Honeybee Sanctuary is **a place where the honeybees can live and thrive, safe from exploitation** and mindless exploration into "whatever is possible, try it." The question "How much honey do you get from your bees?" urgently needs to be revised into **"What do the honeybees need to become and stay strong enough to withstand the onslaught of our modern time** with all the visible and invisible damaging agents?"

Their present loss in vitality and reduced capability of survival is not only caused by conventional agricultural practices with their monocultures and poisons, but also by **our attempt to make beekeeping as profitable as possible** which has driven and shaped our practices for over 100 years.

Take a look at their site if you want to explore further. Be sure to click on their gallery (Look under the tab called The Bees) for some gorgeous photos.

I made a donation – there's a big orange button at the top of their website. I hope you'll consider doing the same. Places like Spikenard need to be encouraged.

BeeAttitude for Day #454: *Blessed are those who let bees be, for they shall hear our song and be comforted.*

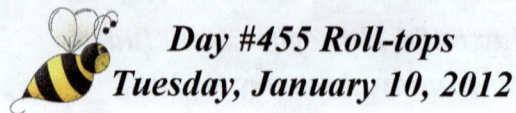

Day #455 Roll-tops
Tuesday, January 10, 2012

When I was a kid, the only roll-top I knew of was an old desk.

So I was intrigued recently when someone sent me a link to a site that shows a rolled-up computer. Who knows where technology is going to lead us over the next few years? When I went to the site, myrolltop.com, one of the first thoughts I had was that if the computer had been yellow instead of silvery (or blue or green or red—so far I've seen videos with all those different colors), it would have looked like a honeybee with those stripes along the body of it.

I know – that's stretching it a bit. You have to use your imagination. Okay, a LOT of imagination!

Part of me thinks the site is a hoax. If so, it's a pretty impressive one. The other part of me thinks, Why not? *[2019 Note: As of today, they still haven't actually produced a rolltop computer. In fact, the last update to their website seems to have been made in 2011. But they're still seeking donations. Don't think I'll jump on that bandwagon.]*

What do you think? If this is real, will it catch on? Is it like the bumblebee that isn't supposed to be able to fly, because scientists can prove that the bumblebee body is too heavy for its wings to support? The people who are developing this roll top computer may be the bumblebees of this generation.

BeeAttitude for Day #455: *Blessed are those who try new flower patches, for they shall be pleasantly surprised.*

Day #456 Australian Adventure
Wednesday, January 11, 2012

For the next few days, I'd like to share a vicarious adventure. My son is in Australia, and his Facebook page is chock full of amazing photographs. He has that "photographer's eye" that seems inborn, the results are so natural.

In my entire life I've taken only three really good photographs – one in London, and two in Vermont. But Eli doesn't have to work at it. The stunning pictures flow out of his camera like an aria out of the mouth of Beverly Sills.

In addition to the photos, he occasionally sums one up with a haiku. So, here's one of his photos of a termite mound that was taller than he was. Enjoy it!

Haiku on Australian outback mysteries (by Eli Reiman):

> miles of fire-ravaged
> sage brush, hawks, and termite towers:
> yet green life bursts forth!

I'll have another photo for you tomorrow.

BeeAttitude for Day #456: *Blessed are those who share beauty, for they shall radiate wonder.*

Day #457 A Spectacular New Year's Eve
Thursday, January 12, 2012

Have you ever wanted to spend a spectacular New Year's Eve? Well, Eli Reiman did this year – he spent it at Uluru in Australia. Here's a picture he took at sunset. Such a magical place -- what a start to a new year!

Uluru at Sunset © 2011 Eli Reiman

I hope you started your New Year as beautifully as Eli did.

Now have a good day today. You might want to join this little guy and have something yummy to munch!

© 2011 Eli Reiman

BeeAttitude for Day #457: *Blessed are those who respect the sacred places on this earth, for Mama Nature shall respond in kind.*

Fran Stewart

Day #458 Clouds
Friday, January 13, 2012

While I'm sharing vicarious Australian journeyings, I simply have to show you this sunset Eli captured in Northern Australia.

© 2012 Eli Reiman

Did you ever notice that **in order to have a lovely sunset, you have to have some clouds**?

Without clouds, the sun just disappears below the horizon, and that's it.

Next time I'm up against clouds in my life, I plan to look for the sunset in them. They have to be there. Mama Nature (and Eli Reiman) tell me so.

In tomorrow's blog I'll explain what Eli does with clouds in his life.

BeeAttitude for Day #458: *Blessed are those who love the wind, for they shall have music around them.*

 ## Day #459 Eli's Clouds Turned to Beauty
Saturday, January 14, 2012

So, yesterday I talked about the necessity of clouds for beautiful sunsets.

Shortly after Eli arrived in Australia, while he was SCUBA diving, someone smashed the back window of his rental car and stole a great deal of specialized camera equipment.

The police officer who came to the scene found a torn woven bracelet, the kind worn by many of the native people of Australia. Eli was introduced rather vividly to the distrust and downright anger of the Aborigines.

He could have railed against his misfortune. He could have turned to hatred. Instead he wrote this haiku:

>lives like shattered glass
>harsh social truths create strife
>why else would he rob?
>—Eli Reiman

and he turned anger into understanding, clouds into a sunset. A good lesson for all of us.

BeeAttitude for Day #459: *Blessed are those who focus on the sunset, for their lives shall reflect beauty.*

BeesKnees #5: A Beekeeping Memoir

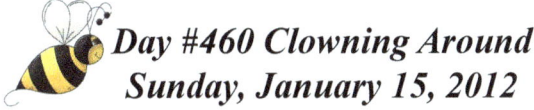

Day #460 Clowning Around
Sunday, January 15, 2012

I know I've been talking/writing about the Australian adventure, but I'd like to digress for today to share with you a photo that one of our loyal blog followers, AggiePete from Houston, shared with me.

Her mother worked for the USO during WWII, and was lucky enough to be in the right place at the right time. She met **Emmett Kelly**, the man who epitomized the world of clowning. Mr. Kelly took clowning to a new level of professionalism.

And here he is:

Whoops! No, that's not Emmett Kelly! That's Eli.

Here›s the real Emmett Kelly:

Let a little laughter into your life today. The bees and I will be happy you did!

BeeAttitude for Day #460: *Blessed are those who save old photos, for they shall keep us all humble and happy.*

BeesKnees #5: A Beekeeping Memoir

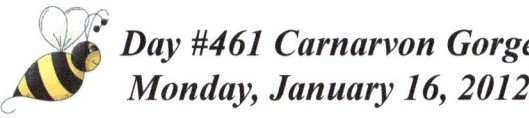

Day #461 Carnarvon Gorge
Monday, January 16, 2012

Here's the last of the Australia photos that I plan to show you. Come to think of it – it might not be the last one. It's simply the last one I've saved so far, but who knows what's around the corner?

This is Carnarvon Gorge. It's part of a national park in central Queensland, Australia. I learned (from Wikipedia, of course) that the canyon is 30 kilometers long, and at the mouth of the gorge, it's 600 meters deep. That's pretty impressive.

As I read on, though, I found that there are concerns about the way tourists hand-feed the animals, causing a population explosion among them and then near-starvation when the humans leave at the end of the tourist season, and the over-populated animals are left to try to find enough food.

Doggone it, why can't people play nicely?

In the meantime, I want to share with you that **something wonderful happened yesterday**, and I'll be writing about it in a couple of days. I need to process it for a while before I'll feel comfortable telling you about it. But I'll give you a hint. It has to do with someone who weighs 1,200 pounds.

BeeAttitude for Day #461: *Blessed are those who leave us alone to live the way we were intended to live, so we can make all the honey we want to.*

Fran Stewart

Day #462 Comet Lovejoy
Tuesday, January 17, 2012

From Australia to the stars. You see, we're not really leaving Australia yet, because this story from NASA Science News contains a photo of Comet Lovejoy that was taken from – would you believe it? – **Poocher Swamp** in South Australia.

Dec 25, 2011 by Wayne England

https://science.nasa.gov/science-news/science-at-nasa/2012/12jan_cometlovejoy/

As fascinated as I am with the story of the comet, I was equally intrigued by the name of the swamp, so I went online to find out about it and found this fascinating tidbit on Wikipedia:

Once owned by Dalton Staude, Poocher Swamp was sold to the Australian Parks and Wildlife Service for a recreation area and is now a favourite spot for pickincking, boating, fishing, yabbying and canoeing.

I get the part about pickincking (typos happen), but what, I ask you is yabbying?

If you find out …

[**2019 Note:** yabbying *means fishing for yabbies, an Australian crayfish-like animal.*]

Oh dear, that phrase reminds me of a gentleman I met in the London tube station long ago. I was trying to get from where I was to another subway station on a different line, and the map of the subway showed that there was an underground walkway between the two. I couldn't find this end of it, though. I walked up to this man, who, in a gray three-piece suit, with a bowler hat in one hand and—I kid you not—an umbrella over his arm, looked the epitome of London gentlemanliness.

I explained what my problem was. "Could you tell me how I get from here," I pointed to the map, "to there?"

He looked at my map, sighed, and said, "Madam, I have lived in London for all of my 63 years, and I have never known how to get from here to there. If you find the answer, do let me know." At which point he stepped into a subway car and was swept away.

I finally found the way, but he was gone.

BeeAttitude for Day #462: *Blessed are those who ask, for they shall—eventually—get answers.*

Fran Stewart

Day #463 Daisy at the Horse Farm
Wednesday, January 18, 2012

Two days ago I told you that something wonderful had happened. If you've read this blog for any length of time, you may have noticed that ever since I decided to take up beekeeping, I've become braver and braver. After all, beekeepers are incredibly brave people. They face thousands of potential stings (and the possibility of actual stings) every time they open a hive.

So actually getting the bees was a first step toward courage.

Lately I've started voice lessons AND an exercise program – both of which took me beyond my comfort zone.

And two days ago, I tackled my fear of horses. I've always been afraid of them, afraid of being stepped on or pinned against a wall, or slammed into by a head as heavy as a sledgehammer. You may recall I wrote about this fear back on Day #430.

But I know a psychotherapist who works with the horses at "Flying Change"—the horses serve as co-therapists to help people work through their various issues. I could think of a few issues it might be time for me to tackle, but the thought of doing it in the company of a potentially lethal half-ton four-legged creature was, shall we say, a bit daunting.

Enter Daisy, a 21-year old mare who lost an eye last year. Sunday afternoon I drove to the other side of Atlanta (about 50 miles from my house), spent half an hour or so talking with Jerry Connor, the therapist, about what I wanted to accomplish, and then we walked down to see Daisy.

I'd met her once before when I accompanied a friend I'll call Donna, who was having a session with Jerry and Google. While Donna was patting Google, I happened to be standing next to a stall where an incredibly gentle horse (Daisy) put her head over the wall and practically begged me to pat her neck. As long as she was on THAT side of the wall and I was on THIS side, it was okay.

So, later, when I called Jerry to make an appointment, I asked if I could work with Daisy.

Sunday, it took me a while to get up the nerve to step into her stall with her, and I stayed near the open door at first. Daisy had been playing in the field and was muddy, muddy, muddy. The mud had dried into her hair. They handed me a stiff flat rubber brush, and I went to work.

Daisy must have enjoyed the scrubbing because at one point she lowered her head and butted into me, scratching the front of her face up and down my wooly vest. It startled me and sort of scared me, until I heard the laughter from the other side of the stall. "That means she likes you and trusts you!"

At one point, Daisy sidled closer to me, and my fear level skyrocketed, as I was between her and the wall of the stall at this point. "You can push her away," I was told, but I didn't believe it. "Just put your hands firmly against her and apply pressure. Don't let up, just keep gently pushing against her. When she realizes you mean it, she'll move."

And, guess what? I did, and she did. I moved a 1,200-pound horse just by setting a boundary. This is my space, and you can't move into it.

Golly day, I wish I'd learned that lesson when I was five. Then maybe I would have remembered it when I was 20, 30, 40, 50.

I came away from the Daisy session feeling so successful, I'm going back for another round next month.

BeeAttitude for Day #463: *Blessed are those who help others to learn, for they shall make the world a better place.*

BeesKnees #5: A Beekeeping Memoir

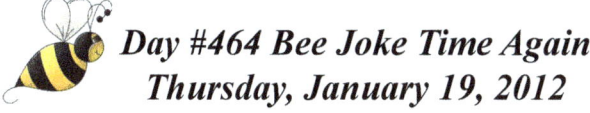
Day #464 Bee Joke Time Again
Thursday, January 19, 2012

Inspired by the recent Australian jaunt:

What do you get when you cross a **bee** with a **boomerang**?

Let's see who wins this one...

BeeAttitude for Day #464: *Blessed are those who like to chuckle, for their insides shall be massaged with laughter.*

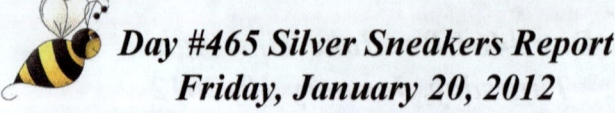

Day #465 Silver Sneakers Report
Friday, January 20, 2012

I've been taking the Silver Sneakers classes now for three full weeks, and I thought you'd like a progress report.

The first day I barely made it through the class, as I've already mentioned.

By the end of the first week, I had a pretty good routine down. I'd take the class, then get on the treadmill and walk one mile, keeping my heart rate at about 135 for a good cardio workout. It took me a little over 26 minutes to walk the mile.

Last Friday (after two weeks of classes), I could do the mile in 22 minutes, AND I'd increased the incline from 1 (wimpy) to 4. Love those readouts!

This week I'm still using only 1-pound weights during the classes, and I'm still doing the "beginner" phase of all the exercises. I still have to hold onto a chair back for most of the balance routines, but I'm not quite as exhausted by the end of class.

The treadmill's getting a bit easier, too. I'm not pushing it too much, just trying to keep my heartbeat at a steady 130 beats per minute. The 135 was just a bit much, so I was smart enough to back off a bit.

A couple of days ago, I did the mile in a few seconds over 20 minutes.

So, this is turning out to be a good decision.

BeeAttitude for Day #465: *Blessed are those who find the best nectar and pollen, for they shall reap the benefits.*

Day #466 Lion Cub
Saturday, January 21, 2012

A friend of mine – someone I've never met in person, but got used to talking to when I called for blood donation appointments – sent me a link to a video of a guy whose last day of work involved getting kissed by the lion cubs he'd been caring for.

As I watched it, it brought to mind something I hadn't thought about in years. Here's the email I sent her in reply:

Pat, what a sweet way to start my day. Thank you for sharing this. Boy, did it bring back wonderful memories.

When I was in 8th grade, my sister came home from college one weekend with four of her friends, and we all went to the Cheyenne Mountain Zoo, which perches on the side of the mountain above Colorado Springs. It was mid-winter, so there weren't a lot of other visitors. Imagine having a whole zoo to oneself!

At any rate, when we got to the aviary, we spread out looking at the various birds. Suddenly, a baby lion came padding into the center of the room, soon followed by one of the keepers, a rather good-looking young man, or so my sister told me later. I wouldn't have known. All I was interested in was the lion cub.

The keeper told us that the various workers took turns socializing the cub, taking him with them as they worked around the zoo. He'd forgotten, apparently, to latch the door, and the cub took advantage of his lapse.

We ended up sitting in a big circle on the floor of the aviary, the girls listening to stories of zoo work from the fellow, while the cub pranced his way around the circle, making friends with everyone. When he got to me, he stayed, probably because I was the only one truly paying attention to him. I received the kinds of hugs and kisses this video shows. My cub was smaller, younger than the ones here, and the only "video" I have of that long-ago event is the one running in my head.

Thank you, Pat, for you inadvertently gave me a delightful gift – the gift of a marvelous memory!

Photo Credit: Pixabay.com

Those little round ears and the scratchy, scratchy tongue still live, and I'm sorry the memory has been buried for so long, but what fun to bring it to light!

BeeAttitude for Day #466: *Blessed are those who share delightful experiences, the way we bees tell each other of good nectar sources, for they shall have wonderful memories forever.*

Day #467 Until the Sled Dogs Sing
Sunday, January 22, 2012

I try not to complain about the weather. I figure the only things I have a right to complain about are the things I helped to institute—or tried to prevent. That's why I vote each year, so I'll earn the right to comment on what is (or isn't) happening on the political scene.

That's why I conserve water, recycle, give blood, and donate to libraries. So I'll have the right to complain if things don't go well – or congratulate myself when they do. After all, I own a piece of the action.

But I don't complain about the weather, since there is absolutely nothing I can do about it. That ridiculous bumper sticker that says Prevent Global Warming, for instance. Just how am I as an individual supposed to prevent global warming? I reduce, reuse, recycle. I buy local products as much as possible. I drive a fuel-efficient car, and I lump all my errands together so I don't have to make repeated trips down the same road.

Still, I'm up against large industries spewing out fossil fuel residues by the ton. And I'm up against the Arctic Oscillation. Not much I can do about that.

What is the Arctic Oscillation? I'm glad you asked. Dauna Coulter, a writer for NASA Science News—I've quoted her before in this blog—explained it quite well this past week. Here's the email that came to me, since I subscribe to NASA Science News:

Winter seems to have been on hold this year in some parts of the United States. Snowfall has been scarce in places that were overwhelmed with the white stuff at the same time last year. In today's story from Science@NASA, climatologist Bill Patzert explains what's going on.

The more I find out about this stuff, the more I realize I have absolutely nothing to complain about.

BeeAttitude for Day #467: *Blessed are those who try to understand the "why" of it all, for they shall find new fields of flowers to explore.*

Day #468 Bee Wisdom and Eli's Blog
Monday, January 23, 2012

Bees are up against a lot of dangers. Sometimes it can be the weather, as I wrote about yesterday. Warm weather like we've been having makes the bees want to fly outside, but there's no nectar or pollen for them to collect, so they waste a lot of energy for no results.

Sometimes they're picked off by a hungry bird. Sometimes their little wings wear out and they can't make it home to the hive. Sometimes a skunk or a bear raids the hive—skunks to eat the bees—bears to eat the honey.

As far as I know, bees don't wage senseless war. Why am I thinking about these things?

Well, for some unknown reason, I went back the other day to take a look at my son's blog. Now, keep in mind that the last time he posted anything was in April of 2006, shortly after three terrorist bombs went off in a marketplace in Dahab, Egypt.

Eli was there, vacationing. He'd been in the marketplace drinking juice, but he wandered away to a restaurant. Then the bombs went off—near the juice bar where he'd been standing minutes before.

The Egyptian government shut down all Internet traffic, so it was almost two days before I knew whether my son was alive. The email I got from him said, "Alive. More later."

[2019 note: The pictures I describe in this paragraph have all been removed from his blog. In fact, there's not a lot left of it, so I'm not going to send you there. I am, however including all of what I wrote in my BeesKnees blogpost.]

The next email began, "I carried dead bodies yesterday." He ended up using parts of that email on his blog. I must warn you that there are pictures (beginning on about the third entry down the page) of the extreme devastation caused by those bombs in April of 2006, including one of the mangled body of a man Eli tried to save. There are also pictures of the hundreds of people who took to the streets the next day begging for peace, demanding that the terrorists stop.

Eli stayed in Dahab for several days afterwards, doing his small part to help the local economy that depended on the tourists (the tourists who left the city in droves after the bombings). Then he went to Israel, where he posted his last blog entry for that year (and the next six years, come to think of it).

He wasn't too excited about traveling for quite a while after that.

Why do we (the collective we of humanity) do such things? Bees are considerably smarter than we are in this aspect.

BeeAttitude for Day #468: *Blessed are those who never treat the world or each other in any way they wouldn't want to be treated themselves.*

Fran Stewart

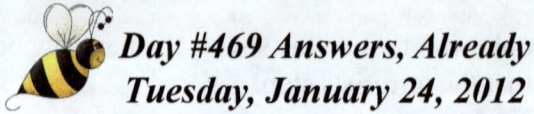

Day #469 Answers, Already
Tuesday, January 24, 2012

Questions are wonderful, aren't they? You know why? It's because asking a question seems to imply that there is probably an answer, and if the answer isn't known yet, it might be worth looking for.

When I ask the bee-joke questions, I don't always have an answer in mind. I just enjoy seeing what you come up with. Sometimes I do have an answer available, but the ones you come up with are frequently funnier than mine.

"*Why*" is one of the most adventuresome words in the English language. Look at where it leads. To outer space, to the depths of the ocean, to the correcting of social ills, to the discovery of new technology.

And sometimes it drives the mothers of four-year-olds absolutely batty.

But still, it's worth asking, don't you think?

And if you're wondering what you get when you cross a bee with a boomerang, the answer might be:

from Texas: "Crocodile DunBee"

from Minnesota: "I dunno, but it's gonna BEE home before you know it"

from Alabama: "An insect that never has to fly backwards"

From Colorado: "A BoomBeeRang"

from New Hampshire: "An AborigiBee," or

from somewhere unidentified: "A circular Buzz saw."

Why do I ask these questions?

Why not?

BeesKnees #5: A Beekeeping Memoir

BeeAttitude for Day #469: *Blessed are those who buzz for the fun of it, for their singing shall brighten the world.*

Fran Stewart

Day #470 Six Words Changed My Attitude
Wednesday, January 25, 2012

Several years ago I was doing a book signing at a bookstore in North Georgia. At one point, the number of customers had slowed to a trickle, then to a standstill. The owner took the opportunity to talk to me about a series of books she loved.

"You have to read them, Fran," she told me, and went on to give a summary of the plot of Hunger Games, the first book in the trilogy. I made some polite noises, but closed my mind to the book. You have to read them, Fran – six words I happily ignored, because the thought of reading a book about a repressive government that forced selected children to fight to the death once a year sounded about as interesting as a root canal.

She went on to replay the plot of the second book (at that time the third one hadn't come out yet), but it still didn't strike my fancy. "You just have to read them," she told me again. Six more words that fell on deaf ears.

But then my granddaughter, Savannah, said a slightly different six words: "I wish you'd read it, Grannie." She'd just finished telling me how much she'd enjoyed that first book and wanted to discuss it with me. But there was nothing to discuss, since I hadn't read it. Until she made her request.

There's a big difference, wouldn't you agree, between **you have to** and **I wish you would**.

The upshot of all this is that I bought Hunger Games by Suzanne Collins for my brand new Kindle and thoroughly enjoyed reading it. Now I can't wait to discuss it with the one who talked me into it in the first place.

BeeAttitude for Day #470: *Blessed are those who persuade with gentle, honeyed words, for their buzz shall be listened to.*

Day #471 Weeds, Wildflowers, and Birdsong
Thursday, January 26, 2012

Here's a thought that came to my inbox from the Daily OM:

"A plant is a weed only within a certain context; one person's weed is another person's wildflower."

I sure will be glad to see honeybees (and bumblebees) in my weedy – whoops! I mean my **wildflower-filled** yard again. That reminds me of a poem I read somewhere or other that was talking about the flow of the seasons. It contained this line:

Oh, that's the reason a bird can sing;

On the darkest day, it believes in Spring.

I wish I knew who wrote that so I could give credit where credit is certainly due.

BeeAttitude for Day #471: *Blessed are those who sing for the fun of it, for they shall spread joy and have it bounce right back to them.*

[**2019 Note:** I googled the first line and found the answer. Look at the next page:]

Fran Stewart

You have to believe in happiness,
Or happiness never comes.
I know that a bird chirps none the less
When all that he finds is crumbs.

You have to believe the buds will blow,
Believe in the grass in the days of snow.
Ah, that's the reason a bird can sing,
On his darkest day he believes in Spring.

You have to believe in happiness—
It isn't an outward thing.
The Spring never makes the song, I guess,
As much as the song the Spring.

Aye, many a heart could find content
If it saw the joy on the road it went,
The joy ahead when it had to grieve,
For the joy is there—but you have to believe.

—Douglas Malloch (1877–1938)

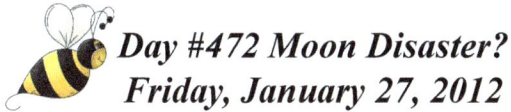 Day #472 Moon Disaster?
Friday, January 27, 2012

Someone recently called my attention to the National Archives. I've used the archives (www.archives.gov) to obtain transcriptions of the Declaration of Independence and the U.S. Constitution, but I hadn't thought much about some of the lesser-known items that are held there.

Here's one goody I came across. I'm old enough to remember sitting in front of a TV set late into the night in July of 1969 to see Neil Armstrong step onto the surface of the moon.

One background bit of information I have never known, however, was the contingency plan for what the President was to have said in case the astronauts were somehow stranded there, unable to return to Mother Earth.

It seems that William Safire, author of the widely syndicated newspaper column *On Language*, was asked to draft a speech, just in case Nixon needed to inform the world that our astronauts were doomed.

Here, copied straight from the national archives, is the text of that speech, followed by Safire's instructions to the president.

= = = = = = = = = =

To: H. R. Haldeman

From: Bill Safire   July 18, 1969

IN THE EVENT OF MOON DISASTER:

 Fate has ordained that the men who went to the moon to explore in peace will stay on the moon to rest in peace.

 These brave men Neil Armstrong and Edwin Aldrin, know that there is no hope for their recovery. But they also know that there is hope for mankind in their sacrifice.

These two men are laying down their lives in mankind's most noble goal: the search for truth and understanding.

They will be mourned by their families and friends; they will be mourned by their nation; they will be mourned by the people of the world; they will be mourned by a Mother Earth that dared send two of her sons into the unknown.

In their exploration, they stirred the people of the world to feel as one; in their sacrifice, they bind more tightly the brotherhood of man.

In ancient days, men looked at stars and saw their heroes in the constellations. In modern times we do much the same, but our heroes are epic men of flesh and blood.

Others will follow, and surely find their way home. Man's search will not be denied. But these men were the first, and they will remain foremost in our hearts.

For every human being who looks up at the moon in the nights to come will know that there is some corner of another world that is forever mankind.

PRIOR TO THE PRESIDENT'S STATEMENT:

The President should telephone each of the widows-to-be.

AFTER THE PRESIDENT'S STATEMENT, AT THE POINT WHEN NASA ENDS COMMUNICATION WITH THE MEN:

A clergyman should adopt the same procedure as a burial at sea, commending their souls to "the deepest of the deep," concluding with the Lord's Prayer.

= = = = = = = = = =

The young daughter of a friend of mine has decided that she wants to be on the first manned flight to Mars. Ever since she was six years old, that has been her goal.

I wonder who will be asked to write the contingency-plan speech for that event...

BeeAttitude for Day #472: *Blessed are those who appreciate the ones who have gone before, for the path they fly will be more sure as a result.*

Day #473 The Problem with Caller ID
Saturday, January 28, 2012

It used to BEE, every phone call was a surprise.

It used to BEE, when I came home after a few hours, and found a blank answering machine, I could say, "Well, probably a lot of people called, but they didn't leave a message."

Ever since I got caller ID, though, I've had to face the indisputable knowledge that not only did nobody leave a message, but nobody called in the first place.

I know the trend went from phone calls to emails to facebook to texting to tweets, but I have to admit I miss phone calls on those days when I don't hear from anyone at all.

Don't get me wrong – emails are great. But there's just something about talking to a real voice that can't be BEEat. The only thing better is having lunch face-to-face with a friend, with cell phones turned off or ignored during the meal.

This afternoon I'll BEE doing just that – and I'm looking forward to it.

If you call while I'm eating, even if you don't leave a message, I'll BEE able to call you back later, BEEcause AT&T will tell me who you are...

BeeAttitude for Day #473: *Blessed are those who leave water in a safe place for us bees, for they shall have the benefit of our buzzing every sunny day.*

BeesKnees #5: A Beekeeping Memoir

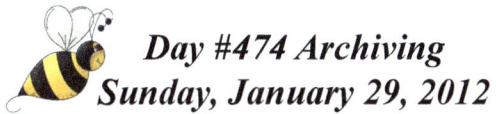
Day #474 Archiving
Sunday, January 29, 2012

Remember that lunch I mentioned yesterday? Well, I had it Saturday afternoon - a lunch with Pat Gerard, who is an archivist. She had spoken to me a couple of years ago about the possibility of archiving my papers.

"Who'd want them?" was my first thought.

But she's convinced me that archiving for future scholars and researchers would be a good idea. After all, someone writing a historical mystery 200 years from now could pick up all sorts of facts about day-to-day life around the turn of the 21st century just by reading my journals.

When I read books about life in the 13th century, I want to know the writer has done her research so she gets all the minutiae right. Someday, my journals may help someone who's writing about those days long ago at the end of the 20th century.

So, I pulled out all my old journals, college papers, lesson plans from when I did community teaching in a grade-school, family photographs (all of which I have to label!), and the transcripts of my grandparents and great-grandmother's diaries.

Pat looked everything over, took some measurements ("How many inches tall would this stack of journals be?"), asked lots of questions, and then we went to lunch at Macaroni Grill.

During lunch she said that she's already started the archiving process for my blog - printing each post on archival paper. This blog, after all, has in a way taken the place of the daily journal entries I used to write.

For the past dozen years or so, I've limited myself to nightly journal jottings that read like a list of what-did-Frannie-do-today. Not very interesting. The older journals, the true ones – the ones where I was agonizing over how to order my life – no longer seemed necessary once I was writing my life and my concerns into my Biscuit McKee mysteries.

Fran Stewart

Just think of it. Some day your great-great-great grandniece might come across the old Stewart papers and glean some sort of wisdom from them.

Wouldn't that be nice?

BeeAttitude for Day #474: *Blessed are those who eat with friends, for they shall digest thoughts as well as food.*

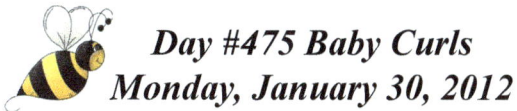
Day #475 Baby Curls
Monday, January 30, 2012

This archiving business is turning up some amazing finds.

Now, maybe you're more organized than I am, so you'll think I'm a slob when I tell you all the goodies I'm finding stuffed in the back of closets.

Things like my baby book. I'd forgotten I even had one. Little tendrils of golden baby curls. A picture of my grandmother sitting in her rocking chair, combing her hair before bedtime. My high school diploma (still don't know what happened to the ones from college—I'll find them someday). Photos of my big sister sitting with me up on the roof.

I still haven't found the big metal box filled with slides. That was what I was looking for when I came across the baby book and all these other treasures.

What I'd really like to know, though, is the last name of the young orderly who took care of me for the first four or five days of my life. All I know is that his name was Tony, and he never left me alone the entire time my mother was out of it. I firmly believe he was an angel in disguise, making sure I could sense that I was wanted, at least for those first few days.

Later that week, my mother finally woke up from all the medication she'd been given and found out I was a girl rather than the boy she had expected.

"But, we can't have a boy," she said. "I don't have a boy's name picked out."

"Don't you worry; I have it all taken care of," my father told her—probably the only time in their whole life together that he got the final say-so.

So, if you know someone named Tony—he would be in his eighties now—who served in a field hospital in California in the late forties, tell him thank you for me. Then email me so I can go visit him.

Fran Stewart

BeeAttitude for Day #475: *Blessed are those who are open to finding treasures when least expected, for they shall have bright days and large smiles.*

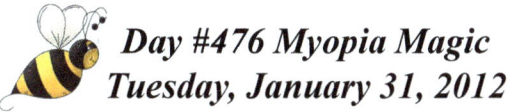 Day #476 Myopia Magic
Tuesday, January 31, 2012

Did you ever put down your glasses and then not be able to find them because, being nearsighted, you can't SEE them?

Photo Credit: Eli Reiman

Today I learned a magic trick from one of those ubiquitous newsletters that seem to circulate indefinitely. I'm sure the tip will help me – and it might help you, too.

Use the camera in your smart phone. Walk around your house looking at the view through the camera lens, and your house will appear in clear definition. That way you can find those glasses quickly and easily.

Of course, I so seldom take my glasses off, and I certainly tend not to set them down unless I'm absolutely sure where they are.

See? There's a distinct advantage to being **way** nearsighted, rather than just sort of nearsighted.

But, if I ever DO lose my glasses, I'll know precisely how to put my phone to work for me.

BeeAttitude for Day #476: *Blessed are those who learn from others, for they shall fly through life more easily.*

Day #477 One more month to plan
Wednesday, February 1, 2012

Golly day, are you going to be impressed in about a month. I met yesterday with a professional about a new website design.

I've been trundling along with a very amateur site for almost ten years, and it's about time for a change, wouldn't you say?

As of right now, I have no idea what it's going to look like, but it should be unveiled by the first week in March.

I'm trying to decide which areas of my current website need to be kept, and which can be tossed. Do I, for instance, really need to have on there a description of every cat I've ever shared a home with?

BeeAttitude for Day #477: *Blessed are those who voice their opinion through voting, for they shall maintain the right to complain later on.*

[**2019 Note from Fran:** Websites and I simply don't go together, I guess. I've gone through three different ones since this particular iteration, none of which I can keep up myself. Therefore, they're out of date as soon as a new book comes out. Stick to my FranStewartAuthor Facebook page. It's a lot more current.]

 Day #478 New Twist on an Old Cliché
Thursday, February 2, 2012

My friend Lisa Washington, who created B'Tyli, a gentle line of skin care and beauty products, came up with a great new twist.

[2019 Note: Lisa has since transferred her energies to raw foods and healthy living. Here's her new website: Set The Table With Love. The old site is no longer available.] In a Facebook post yesterday she said she was no longer going to

kill two poor little birds with one stone.

Instead, she was going to

set free two birds with one key .

Isn't that a lovely thought?

I hope it catches on. Birds need all the help they can get.

Lisa is the reason I give to the **American Kidney Fund** by the way. I'm so glad she's not only well but thriving.

BeeAttitude for Day #478: *Blessed are those who see the world through new eyes, for their bright world shall illuminate the whole hive.*

Day #479 Bees and Flies and Questions
Friday, February 3, 2012

If you open the link in this post, understand that it is not for the faint of heart, particularly if you're squeamish about maggots.

I discovered a report on why some bees are in trouble.

That's not true. I myself did not discover that report. Someone (and I'm sorry to say I can't remember who it was) sent me a link.

The story is of a scientist, Dr. John Hafermik, who got curious about seeing dozens, sometimes hundreds, of dead bees littering the sidewalk near his laboratory at San Francisco State University. Not only were there dead bees, but there were others just wandering around in circles, looking horribly dazed.

He collected one of the dead bees in a little jar, set the vial on his desk, and then forgot about it. A week later, he found the culprit(s) behind the death.

https://www.kqed.org/science/10241/zombees-flight-of-the-living-dead

It's when we ask "Why?" that the magic begins, the answers unroll, and we leave the world (or at least our own lives) richer, more meaningful, as a result.

What will you choose to ask about today?

BeeAttitude for Day #479: *Blessed are those who ask about us bees and then look for answers, for – even though we won't show it directly – we shall be grateful.*

BeesKnees #5: A Beekeeping Memoir

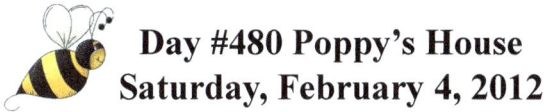
Day #480 Poppy's House
Saturday, February 4, 2012

Every so often, I take off into the woods of North Georgia and visit my friend Polly Hunt Neal, affectionately known as Poppy to her many friends. As I write this on Friday afternoon, to be posted on Saturday at 12:01 a.m., I'm sitting in a gazebo where I wrote the first few pages of INDIGO AS AN IRIS several years ago.

I'd been in a slump at the time – some people call it writer's block. Others say it's lack of inspiration. At any rate, I'd been looking at blank pages for so long, I'd begun to wonder if my muse (whatever or whoever that may have been) had left me.

At any rate, Poppy called me somewhere in the middle of that bleary time and invited me up for the weekend. When I arrived that day, she hadn't returned yet from a quick errand that turned into a longer errand than she'd expected. Not knowing where she was, I wandered out to the gazebo with my notebook and a pencil. I trusted that Poppy would show up soon, although a whiff of concern passed through my mystery-writer's mind when I briefly wondered if she'd been kidnapped.

I was moderately hungry, and the cinnamon bun I'd snitched on the trip up had long gone, so I wrote cinnamon buns at the top of the page, and kept going from there, with the beginning of a story about a kidnapping gone horribly awry.

Of course, Poppy eventually drove in, and I shared with her the beginning of INDIGO.

By the time you read this blog post, I'll be home after two uplifting, relaxing days with Poppy. Every time I come here, I get a lot of writing done – and we eat a lot of honey on biscuits!

Life can't get much better than this.

BeeAttitude for Day #480: *Blessed are those who welcome friends, for they shall shine with shared affection.*

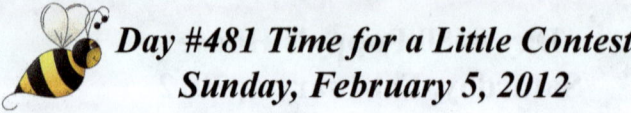
Day #481 Time for a Little Contest
Sunday, February 5, 2012

Petie from Texas, known to readers of this blog as AggiePete, came up with a great idea after she read Thursday's blog (February 2nd).

Let see who can come up with the best twist on the cliché "Kill two birds with one stone."

Or, if you'd rather update a different saying, replacing a negative-sounding cliché with a more positive one, feel free to do so.

Lisa Washington said to set two birds free with one key.

So – what can you come up with?

BeeAttitude for Day #481: *Blessed are those who are open to new and better ideas, for they shall fly through life like us bees (instead of being bogged down like you humans often are).*

Day #482 Speaking of Birdbrains
Monday, February 6, 2012

I got to thinking about the pejorative term *birdbrain*.

There are days when I'd be proud to be called a bird brain. Did you know that chickadees can recall the location of hundreds of seeds they've hidden beneath branches, under tussocks of grass, beneath the edges of mounds of leaves?

Quite a feat.

And I can't remember where I put my green notebook. Wish I had a Bird Brain!

BeeAttitude for Day #482: *Blessed are those who appreciate the value of all creatures, for they shall, perhaps, learn something from them.*

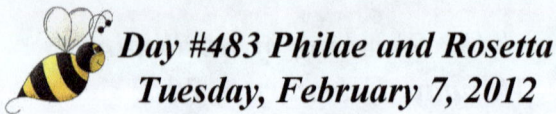 Day #483 Philae and Rosetta
Tuesday, February 7, 2012

My e-friend Dauna Coulter has done it again (as she always does in her articles for **NASA Science News**). She's made a little-known scientific project not only understandable, but lyrical as well.

NASA's **Rosetta Project,** as Dauna explains it, is a romantic plan for landing on a comet (not-so-romantically named **67P**) some time in November of 2014.

Why do I call this a romantic plan? [And I must mention here that romantic was my term for the project, not Dauna's.] I'm glad you asked, though. The lander, the little craft that will descend to the surface of the comet while Rosetta orbits a mere kilometer above, is named **Philae**. Philae is an island in the Nile River, the site of an obelisk that was crucial in the decipherment of the Rosetta Stone.

I just love to read proof not only of the knowledge of scientists, but their literacy as well. And I don't mean that to sound condescending. I'd truly like to meet the person who came up with the Philae/Rosetta tie-in. Just as the Rosetta Stone unlocked the secret language of hieroglyphics, good ole Philae is set to help us decipher the mysteries of what comets are and where (and when) they come from.

Here's where to fnd the whole story, if you're interested:

https://science.nasa.gov/science-news/science-at-nasa/2012/02feb_rosetta/

There's a video version of the story there as well.

BeeAttitude for Day #483: *Blessed are those who fly to new fields, for they shall find nectar in abundance.*

Day #484 Please Send Good Thoughts to My EllieBug
Wednesday, February 8, 2012

So, am I going to write something brilliant this evening?

In a word, one word, No.

Yesterday, on the way home from a local organic farm, where I bought carrots and yummy blackberry yogurt and a few other things as well, my sweet little polka-dotted car died on me. Thank goodness I wasn't in the fast lane of Highway 316 when it happened. I pulled over, let her sit for a few moments, and started her back up.

Called my mechanics – Ray and Dan. Told Ray the service engine soon light had come on when the engine died. "Bring it here now, if not sooner," he said. I called my blessed daughter and asked her to meet me at the shop.

The car stopped again, but once more I pulled over and let it sit a minute before starting up again. As my daughter headed my way, though, up busy Highway 20, she spotted me stopped, for the third time, beside the road. This time a wonderful young man named Tyler stopped to help. He managed to get the battery out and directed us to Reilly's Tire Center, which was just on the other side of the road set back at the end of a shopping center.

Veronica and I drove my battery over there and had it tested. "Dead," the testing machine proclaimed. No, I take that back. It didn't say Dead. It said, "Bad."

Poor little battery. Being judged by a machine.

At any rate, we went back with a new battery to where EllieBug still stood beside the road, placed the battery inside the hood, and couldn't get the blinkin' plastic covers off the terminals. Finally another very kind man took pity on us and searched his car for a screwdriver.

Veronica drove behind me on that final fateful mile and a half. I heaved a huge sigh of relief as I pulled into the shop's driveway.

What's the verdict? No idea. But once I find out, I'll let you know.

Bees are lucky. They never have to worry about batteries or alternators or gears or brakes or broken windshields or empty gas tanks or ...

Of course, they have to worry about marauding birds and skunks and bears and humans ...

I think I'll be happy where I am.

BeeAttitude for Day #484: *Blessed are those who take the time to lend a wing, for they shall feel better about themselves and shall fly straighter as a result.*

BeesKnees #5: A Beekeeping Memoir

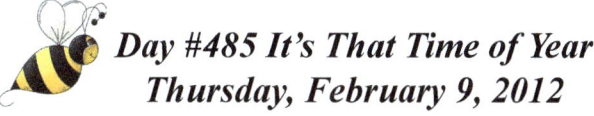
Day #485 It's That Time of Year
Thursday, February 9, 2012

Remember the old song: "It's that time of year, when the world falls in love..."

Wait! No. That songwriter was talking about December. I'm talking about NOW.

In the South, late January and early February is when queen bees start laying eggs, so our song goes: "It's that time of year, when the queens start to lay..." Twenty-one days after she lays those first 2,500 eggs, the babies will hatch, begin their cell-cleaning and comb-building routines. They'll go through all those hive jobs that bees have been doing for millions of years.

Then, a few short weeks later, the bees from hatch #1 will be ready to go out to forage – and by then, there should (hopefully) be some spring growth, with nectar and pollen.

I know this happens every year. But I still can't help marveling at the sheer miracle of it.

Speaking of miracles – EllieBug is back on her feet with not only that new battery, but also a new crankshaft sensor. Thank you for your encouraging emails!

So, Wednesday evening, when I drove to the Gwinnett County training session for precinct managers and assistant managers (I'll be one of the assistant managers at the upcoming March 6th election), I felt perfectly safe in my happy little polka-dotted car.

BeeAttitude for Day #485: *Blessed are those who welcome Spring, for they shall celebrate along with us as we fly in quest of nectar.*

Fran Stewart

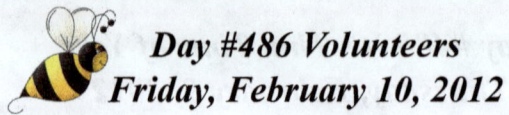

Day #486 Volunteers
Friday, February 10, 2012

Sometimes I think this country runs on volunteers. Yesterday evening I sat through a meeting of the Gwinnett Choral Guild Board of Directors, and I was struck with the level of dedication of those people. All of us believe in the work of the Choral Guild. We come together to sing for the sheer joy of it, and we all love the way our director gives us challenging music to sing.

But, a lot of people in that room last night have been on the Board, in various positions, for years and years. I'm one of them. I happen to believe that I have a responsibility to put in some effort for the groups I want to see succeed.

There are quite a few members of the Guild, though, who see the Guild running quite well day to day, week to week, and probably think that their input isn't necessary. But volunteering is like voting. If you don't do it, you don't have the right to complain!

Well, maybe we'll get them this go-round. It's that time of year when the nominating committee gears up to select a slate of officers for next year.

How about you? Have you looked for ways to volunteer? I'm not talking about running yourself ragged trying to be on every committee ever invented. No. Choose what's important to you – and then why don't you do something to help? Believe me, you'll be appreciated!

BeeAttitude for Day #486: *Blessed are those who nurture the baby bees, for they shall ensure the continuation of the hive.*

Yippee! Happy Birthday,

Percy Brown & Carly Stine

! ! ! ! ! !

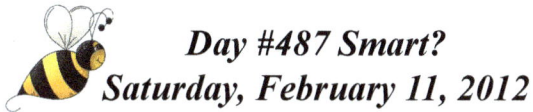

Day #487 Smart?
Saturday, February 11, 2012

You're not going to believe this – or maybe you will.

You may be aware that I'm gradually—very gradually—moving into the 21st century. It's taken me only 12 years to do it.

Last month I bought an iPhone as a birthday present to myself, and I'm getting a new appreciation for the term "smart" phone. This morning I woke up before dawn as usual to take the bird feeders outside. I choose to bring them inside each night because there's a pair of cute little raccoons who delight in climbing the pole and defeating the squirrel baffle. That thing works for squirrels, but not for the longer-armed raccoons.

Usually, I just keep going with my day. I rather enjoy watching the growing light of morning as I eat my breakfast by the bay window. But this morning (it's Friday as I write this blog post), I took out the feeders, fed the cats, and went back to bed, since I'd had only five hours of sleep.

When Miss Polly woke me at 9:00 by stepping across my face, I reached over and picked up my iPhone. When you hit the button three times, a question appears on the screen.

"What can I help you with?"

"I need to laugh, Siri," I said. "Tell me a joke."

Her immediate answer:

"Two iPhones walk into a bar...I forget the rest."

"Thank you, Siri."

"You're welcome."

Well, by the time I made it to the kitchen, I was still chuckling.

I was tempted to ask her for another joke, but I think I'll limit myself to one a day. I do wonder just how many have been programmed into the innards of this "smart" phone. It's not the phone that's smart, though. It's the people who thought all this up in the first place.

Let's hear it for Steve Jobs.

And if Siri repeats herself tomorrow, I'll let you know.

BeeAttitude for Day #487: *Blessed are those who bring their visions to reality, for they shall spread sunshine.*

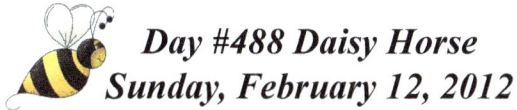 ***Day #488 Daisy Horse***
Sunday, February 12, 2012

Y ou asked for a horse report, so here it comes.

I had my second appointment with Daisy the Horse and Jerry (the therapist) and Lissa (the other therapist and horse owner) in the Flying Change program.

Meeting my fears and doing something about them in a safe environment is, on the one hand, invigorating and, on the other hand, exhausting. I came out of the two-hour session with wobbly legs and shaky hands, but with a big grin.

When I first arrived, I took this picture of some of the other horses up in the pasture, tucked under the overhanging branches of tall pine trees.

Jerry and Lissa weren't there yet, so I took a sneak peek at Daisy. I tried to take a photo of the two of us together.

Daisy has had some problems with one of her back legs, and it's all bandaged up in purple. They use a different color wrap for each day of the week to show that the medication has been put on it that day.

I talked to Daisy for a while, until Lissa showed up with the carrots.

Finish what's in your mouth first, Daisy, and then you can have the rest of this.

You may remember that I told you last month that Daisy had lost an eye. In these pictures you can see the empty socket. When the eyeball was removed, the vet covered the hole with skin stretched from the surrounding tissue, and, although you can't see it in these pictures, the skin has gradually grown hair. So Daisy has a **fuzzy** eye socket.

After I brushed and combed her, we let her out of her stall so she could munch grass in front of the barn – there's an enclosed courtyard there. And I had a chance to approach her when she was out in the open. It felt scarier to me than being in the stall, although I suppose I should have felt safer outside because I could easily move out of her way.

I even got in a hug.

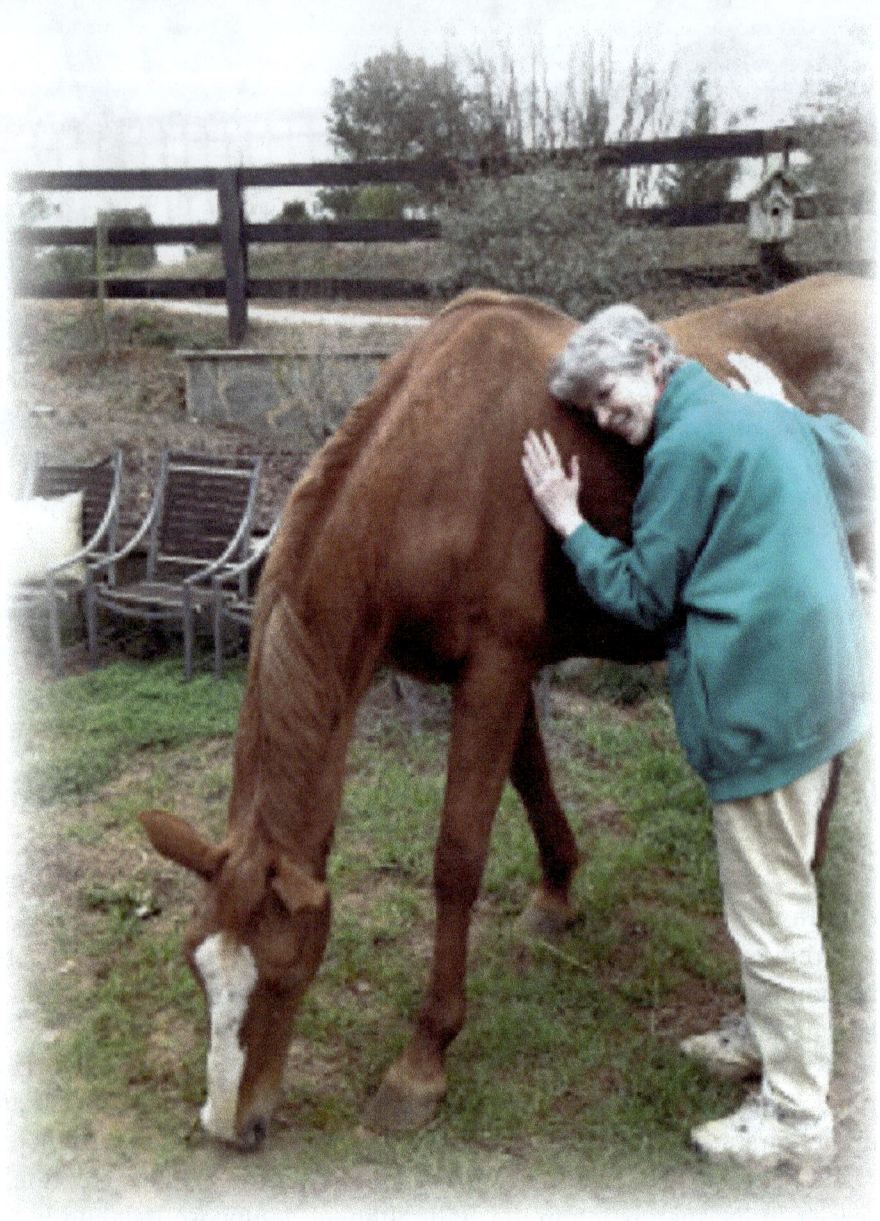

And then Lissa pointed out that Ben, a very young horse, was watching me over the fence, so I worked up my courage to go talk with him. At one point he snuggled his muzzle into the crook of my elbow and just stood there.

Next month I'm going to try to put a halter on Daisy the Horse.

You've been with me through the whole bee process, so you might as well come along on the horse project.

And, I have to show you this: When I got home, Daisy the Cat had a great time sniffing every single finger. She could tell I'd been scratching somebody other than her.

BeeAttitude for Day #488: *Blessed are those who help others allay their fears, for they shall leave the world a better place for their having been here.*

bee.s. my smart phone ain't so smart. She knows only that one joke. Ah well...

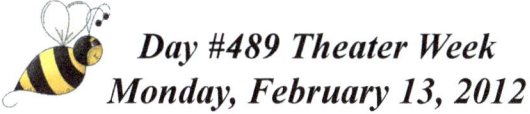

Day #489 Theater Week
Monday, February 13, 2012

What an amazing week this is turning out to be.

Yesterday I went with my friend Millie Woollen to the Aurora Theater in Lawrenceville to see *Body of Water*. I hadn't known anything about the show ahead of time. We both have season tickets, so we just show up regardless of what's playing.

Body of Water turned out to be a moving, disturbing, challenging, funny, sad, excruciating play about memory loss. I came out of it determined more than ever to appreciate each moment of my life.

Later on this week I'll be going to the Atlanta Shakespeare Tavern to see Romeo and Juliet TWICE. The first time will be with my daughter and two of my grandchildren—the two pre-teens. I love watching their enthusiasm over the way the actors carry them along through the story.

And then, a couple of days after that, I'll go back to the Tavern to see the show again with Millie. We both are Club Ticket Holders, which means we see every show there. And, because I like to take my grandkids, sometimes I see the shows twice.

There's something about live theater – good live theater – that simply cannot be explained to someone who's never seen it. I have on occasion seen the same Shakespeare play three or four times in the same month, and it has different nuances every single time. The Shakespeare Tavern is an "Original Practice Playhouse," which means that they perform the plays as Shakespeare's company did, with the actors acknowledging the presence of the audience. That means that the mood of the audience – always a variable from night to night – determines in part how the show "feels" that evening.

If you're ever in the Atlanta area, do yourself a favor. Take in some live theater!

BeeAttitude for Day #489: *Blessed are those who work at what they love, for they shall spread joy in their wake.*

Day #490 You Know What Day It Is?
Tuesday, February 14, 2012

You see, I used to hate Valentine's Day. The reason (I know now after years of working on myself with a great deal of help from some very wise mentors and friends) was that I didn't like myself very much.

All that has changed.

Happy Valentine's Day ! ! ! ! ! ! ! !

I tell my editing clients that they're allowed only one exclamation point per chapter. The «point» (pun intended) is to make the writing powerful enough to eliminate the need for excessive punctuation.

Today, as you can see, I've chosen to make an exception to that rule of mine.

BeeAttitude for Day #490: *Blessed are those who love themselves, for they shall then be able to love others without reservation.*

Day #491 Learning New
Wednesday, February 15, 2012

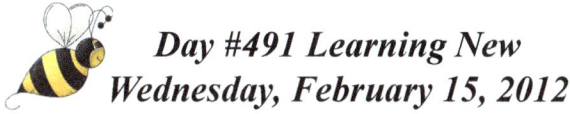

Tuesday evening, the Gwinnett Beekeepers Club had an open forum meeting. That meant there wasn't a regular speaker. Instead, the club president, Tommy Bailey, who served as a mentor to me when I was starting as a beekeeper, answered questions.

Tommy considers himself a "natural" beekeeper. He doesn't medicate his bees, since he's convinced that ultimately weakens the entire bee population. His policy has always been – if a hive is strong, that's great; if a hive is weak, that's too bad. His tendency, he told us, has been to let the weak hives die off.

But now, he's learned a lesson from another beekeeper. It makes so much sense. Here it is:

Photo Credit Timothy Paule II (Pexels.com)

The strength of a hive depends primarily on the genes of the queen. If she's a good layer, then the hive is more likely to survive. If her genes create bees that are capable of fighting off the varroa mite (a major killer of honeybees), then the eggs she lays will hatch into bees that know how to distinguish between larvae that have the varroa mite and ones that don't host the mite. If those bees know what they're doing, they'll kill off the infected larvae, and the hive will thrive.

So – and here's the reasoning that makes so much sense – if a beekeeper has a weak hive, instead of letting it die off, cleaning out the varroa-riddled comb, and introducing a brand new package of bees – instead of that, just put a new, stronger queen in there. Within six weeks, every bee from the old, weak strain will have died off, and all the remaining bees will be from the new genetic strain. They will clean out the larvae that are infected. Voilá! a saved hive.

Just goes to show you, even after years of beekeeping, it's possible to learn earth-shaking new ways. Even after years of being afraid of horses, it's possible to do some re-thinking. Even after years of resentment or anger, it's possible to forgive.

Take your pick. We can all learn something new.

BeeAttitude for Day #491: *Blessed are those who provide us with good houses, for they shall have honey in abundance.*

Day 492 Pollen Time
Thursday, February 16, 2012

Well, it's official. The bees have been collecting pollen here in the metro Atlanta area. The reports are that it's yellow, red, and sort of a bright orange.

The only things I can see blooming in my yard are daffodils, Vinca Minor, and Hellebore, but there must be other flowers out there if other beekeepers are reporting pollen collecting.

The birds are certainly going through mealworms like crazy, which means they're thinking about nesting and egg laying.

Even though it's hard to believe, spring is on its way.

I remember that early **bright, light spring green**. I was first aware of it when I lived in Vermont. After a long, hard winter, suddenly there was one magical day when a wisp of green hovered in the tree branches.

I don't see that so much here in Georgia. Spring is still a magical time, but not quite the same as it was up north. Here Spring oozes up on you; in Vermont it springs forth. Maybe it's just that we longed for Spring a lot more when the weather had been dropping below freezing on a regular basis.

BeeAttitude for Day #492: *Blessed are those who appreciate all the seasons, for they shall be aware of life, and life shall surprise them beautifully.*

Fran Stewart

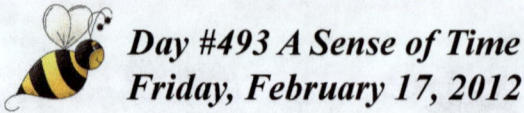

Day #493 A Sense of Time
Friday, February 17, 2012

Years ago, if people wanted to know what time it was, they would look up at the sky. Pre-dawn, dawn, early morning, mid-morning, late morning, midday, and so on through sunset and dusk and twilight and night.

Those estimates were good enough.

The same is true, I would imagine, with bees. With all diurnal animals, for that matter. If it's not yet dawn, the bees stay in the hive. When it's noon (assuming the day is relatively clear) the foragers had better be outside foraging.

But what about the nocturnal animals? How do they tell the difference between 10 pm and 3 am? There's no sun to see the position of. The moon does shift, of course, but it does so on a nightly basis. Can raccoons or bats tell the difference between a gibbous moon and a half-moon, other than the amount of light being spread?

How does the possum visiting the earth at the bottom of my bird-feeding station know s/he has four hours left before daylight?

The trouble with asking questions like this is that, not only do I not know the answers, but I don't even know where to find the answers.

If you know, please enlighten me.

BeeAttitude for Day #493: *Blessed are those who find answers, for they can feel a well-deserved smugness.*

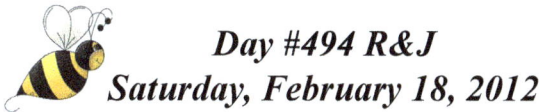

Day #494 R&J
Saturday, February 18, 2012

Friday evening I took two of my grandchildren to the Atlanta Shakespeare Tavern to see Romeo and Juliet. More than 400 years since that play was first performed, and it's still wringing tears from audiences.

Every time I see it, I hear at least two or three lines I could swear I'd never heard before.

I've noticed a change over the years, though. When I was in my twenties and thirties, I got caught up in the tragedy of the story.

In my forties and fifties, I studied the emotional makeup of the various characters.

Now that I'm in my sixties, I want to take those two youngsters and shake them.

- "Tell your father, Juliet. He likes Romeo; he'll holler a bit, and then he'll say okay."

- "Romeo, listen to the Friar, for heaven's sake. 'A pack of blessings light upon your head.' Juliet's alive, you're alive, you've been banished when you could have been executed. All will be well."

Or, all would have been well, if Romeo hadn't gone nuts with useless grief and killed himself.

Of course, if those two teenagers had listened to the voice of reason, we wouldn't have had a play that lasted 400 years.

I guess it's just as well.

BeeAttitude for Day #494: *Blessed are those who write well, for they shall live long through their words.*

 ## Day #495 The Rabbit and Bee Bill
Sunday, February 19, 2012

The Georgia House of Representatives recently passed a bill to prevent local municipalities from passing laws that prohibit Georgia residents from gardening or from keeping honeybees. Here's the text of House Bill 853:

"No county, municipality, consolidated government, or local government authority shall prohibit or require any permit for the growing or raising of food crops, rabbits, honeybees, or chickens, with the exception of roosters, in home gardens, fully covered pens, hives, or fully covered coops on private residential property so long as such food crops, animals, or honeybees or the products thereof are used for human consumption by the occupant of such property and members of his or her household and not for commercial purposes."

The trouble is, the bill is stalled in the State Senate's Rules Committee. If it doesn't make it out of there by March 7th, it's dead, so I've written emails to the various players asking them to support the bill.

Did you notice they're not allowing roosters? I suppose that's a good idea, since roosters aren't necessary for egg production. I rather like the rooster who lives in the lot on the other side of my stream, though. He crows at dawn. He crows whenever he feels threatened (I think). Or maybe when he's happy. He crows just about any time he feels like it. And that's okay with me. Of course, he's not right beside my windows.

How does your local government deal with bees and rabbits and chickens?

And – a very personal note – would you please send prayers, good thoughts, good energy, good vibrations, or whatever you call it, to my niece Erica? She's in the hospital in Colorado, and I'm deeply concerned. I was living with my sister when Erica was born. She's always been a dear person, and I'd like to see her pull through this in the best possible way.

[**2019 Note:** Eri is alive and thriving even as I write this. I'm glad—the world needs her special brand of humor.]

BeeAttitude for Day #495: *Blessed are those who are aware of what is happening around them, for they shall avoid harsh surprises.*

Fran Stewart

Day #496 Some Advice, Please?
Monday, February 20, 2012

I'm getting fed up with my WiFi setup. My house is on the back side of Hog Mountain. Not on the top, mind you, but down a ways, and the land behind me slopes up away from the stream, leaving me in a dip.

People who live farther up the street from me get a fairly good WiFi signal. I don't.

I keep getting ads about bundles and packages – all of them touting that not only will I get high speed internet service, but my TV will never look better. Trouble is, I don't have a TV, don't want one, and don't intend to pay for that kind of service when I don't need it.

Does anybody have some really good advice about how to get good, dependable WiFi service all by itself? Something that will work here on the back side of the mountain?

BeeAttitude for Day #496: *Blessed are those who can live without technology, the way we bees do, for they shall have few headaches.*

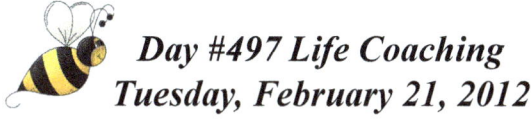
Day #497 Life Coaching
Tuesday, February 21, 2012

As I've told you before, this year is turning out to be one of major soul-searching on my part, and major changes in the way I approach life.

I've shared with you my attempts to overcome my fear of horses, my journey into the worlds of technology, my Silver Sneakers exercise program.

Another bugaboo has reared its head. I signed up for a life-coaching phone session with Jeanette Meierhofer, someone I met years ago at the Shakespeare Tavern. I made the appointment on something of a whim, but the results of it surprised me.

What I hadn't consciously recognized is that I'm afraid of dying. I never, ever thought of myself as dreading the final reaper. I've shared with you how peaceful my father's death was, and how I wanted to choose a death like his, for he showed me that dying could be a conscious, loving choice.

I've always scorned Dylan Thomas and his insistence that one "not go gentle into that good night / rage, rage against the dying of the light."

But, that was when I was in my thirties, forties, fifties. Now that I'm halfway through my sixties, I'm beginning to realize that I might not have as long ahead of me as I thought I'd have.

And I don't wanna go. I want to rage against it.

There are still too many books to be read, too many books to be written, too many places to visit. There are grandchildren to watch grow up, friends to laugh with, songs to sing. Thank goodness I talked with Jeanette about my fears. When we started, she asked me where, on a scale of 1 to 10, my fears lay. I felt like a basket case. My fear was up around a 7 at least. She listened compassionately, asked intelligent questions, and left me with a couple of assignments (should I choose to do them). By the time the appointment was over, my fear level had dropped to a 5.

That felt like a big change to me.

And then I watched the movie *The Children of Chabannes*, a documentary about people who were rescued as children from concentration camps and taken to a school at Chateau Chabannes, in France. These people, the ones still living, were in their seventies, eighties, and nineties, and were still going strong, still living productive lives. What wonderful role models. "Jeanette was right," I told myself. "I don't have to shrivel up. I can keep right on living a productive life."

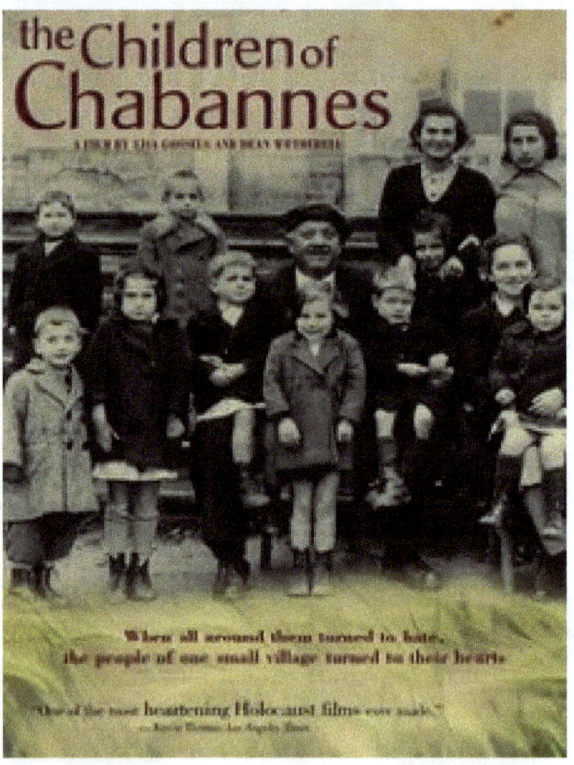

Once I slept on it, I was down to a 3 or 4.

So now, all I have to do … is … do it!

BeeAttitude for Day #497: *Blessed are those who serve as role models and show the rest of the bees how to live, for they shall leave the hive a better place.*

Day #498 Hellebores
Wednesday, February 22, 2012

I haven't seen any bees on the hellebore – yet – but I'm hoping they're getting some nectar from these early flowers.

There was ice on the bird feeder this morning, but it wasn't very thick. I have to admit I have no idea how honeybees, birds, or small animals of any sort manage to make it through long cold winters.

Well, I do know the mechanics of how bees make it through winter—by unhinging their flying muscles and then shivering their wings and bodies to generate heat. But I still don't get it, if you know what I mean.

I think I've gotten awfully spoiled living in Georgia. Of course, in exchange for mild weather, I've given up being able to see the stars at night. Sometimes I think it's worth it. Sometimes I don't.

BeeAttitude for Day #498: *Blessed are those who help the birds, for they shall see joyous feathered flights.*

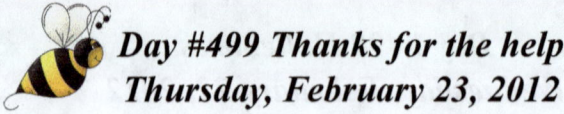 Day #499 Thanks for the help
Thursday, February 23, 2012

Thank you to Petie Ogg and her son Billy, who contacted me with suggestions about WiFi/DSL and such. Yesterday I went to the AT&T booth in the Mall of Georgia and spoke with the manager, who set me up for an installation appointment on March 3rd. The bottom line will save me about $40 each month. Hopefully, this will work.

In the meantime, I'll muddle my way through each day, trying to get this blog posted. It's worked so far, but I'm looking forward to letting go of the daily WiFi struggle. "Push the easy button," to quote you-know-who.

And another thank-you to my dear friend from High School, Ellen Norton, who sent me a tall graceful bottle of pomegranate vinegar that she made herself. How delightful a taste, Ellen.

The bees are beginning to explore, looking for nectar and pollen. For next year I absolutely HAVE to plant more early-blooming shrubs.

BeeAttitude for Day #499: *Blessed are those who liven up their yards with food for us bees, for they shall have the beauty of flowers and the deliciousness of honey.*

Day #500 Five Hundred??????
Friday, February 24, 2012

What is there about list items with a couple of zeros at the end?

When I started this blog in October of 2010 and pledged to write every day for 600 days, I found it hard to believe I'd get to 200 or 300, much less 500.

Some of you have been with me right from the start, some of you are relative newcomers to the BeesKnees Beekeeping Blog, but no matter which category you fit into, I'm grateful for the fact that you choose to spend a part of your day with me, here in the midst of these musings of mine.

Pat Gerard, the archivist who is beginning to catalog my papers, has informed me that this blog holds an important place in my writings. She's printing off each post on archival paper so the collection will have a chance of surviving several hundred years at least.

What on earth will people in the 22nd century think about these ramblings of mine, assuming that someone out there finds them in the course of a research project?

Should I be mindful that I'm writing for posterity? Well, I don't think so. I'm writing for you. And for myself. I'm writing for members of the beekeeping community as well as for people who don't know one end of a bee from another.

I hope that in the course of this journey with me you've learned a little bit about honeybees, a little bit about conservation and ecology, a little bit about approaching life joyously, and a little bit about the value of laughing hard every day.

If you have, I've done my job. I'm awfully glad you're along for the ride!

Fran Stewart

BeeAttitude for Day #500: *Blessed are those who feel the wonder of the world around them, for they shall be endlessly amazed.*

bee.s. from Fran: Thank you for all your encouraging emails about Erica. The good news is that the breathing tube is out, she's been able to say a few words, and her feisty, wonderful self is apparent in those sparkling eyes. We're all breathing a lot easier now – especially her!

www.ingramcontent.com/pod-product-compliance
Lightning Source LLC
Chambersburg PA
CBHW071711020426
42333CB00017B/2219